Helping Church Workers Succeed

The Enlistment and Support of Volunteers

D-B HEUSSER

Judson Press ® Valley Forge

Helping Church Workers Succeed

Copyright © 1980
Judson Press, Valley Forge, PA 19481

Unless otherwise indicated Bible quotations in this volume are from Today's English Version, the *Good News Bible*—Old Testament: Copyright © American Bible Society, 1976; New Testament: Copyright © American Bible Society, 1966, 1971, 1976. Used by permission.

Library of Congress Cataloging in Publication Data

Heusser, D-B
  Helping church workers succeed.

  Bibliography: p.
  1. Church work. 2. Laity. 3. Church management.
I. Title.
BV4400.H4   254   79-24580
ISBN 0-8170-0868-3

Contents

1
Introduction

Because of the thousands of volunteers involved, the church must take seriously the whole concept of volunteerism. Secular volunteer groups have done this for some time, but little meaningful work has been attempted in the area of understanding volunteerism in the church. We, in the church, have assumed that a person will serve, no matter what the position or job, because of a personal commitment to Jesus Christ. A quick glance at most churches will reveal that not all persons have this type of commitment or serve for this reason.

History shows us that volunteerism has always had an important place in the life of the American church. In the New World, the old parish system of congregational life began to break down. Soon there had developed what historians call "the gathered church," that is, a congregation of persons who had "gathered" or joined together in a voluntary association to form a congregation or church. This was in direct contrast to the membership by residence fostered by the parish system found in the Old World. Therefore, churches in America grew from the people and their felt need of fellowship and religious worship. It was this "gathered church" system that also fostered the growth of the "lay-minister." In this situation a noncleric was given, by a congregation, the authority and power to be a minister or pastor to that congregation.

Not only has church membership in the New World been voluntary, but the leadership has also been of a voluntary nature. A major portion of the leaders in the American churches have been and presently are from the ranks of volunteers. The church has been and still is very dependent upon persons who are willing to give leadership, time, and talents with no financial remuneration. Therefore, we can see that volunteerism has been a keynote of the life of the American church. The church in America has had its base in volunteerism!

Today, volunteerism is very much alive in the church. All we need do is look at the educational functions and the various boards, committees, and groups that comprise the organizational structures of the local church or the denomination, and we can see that volunteerism is truly alive! We can say with certainty that the church is dependent upon a volunteer staff far more than on any paid professional staff!

Therefore, it is the basic assumption of this book that:

Volunteers are important persons!

This book is being written to help churches take volunteerism and the volunteer more seriously; to help us who work with volunteers to understand better the needs of those who serve as volunteers; to understand better our function as supervisors working with volunteers; to see how we can assist volunteers with their assignments, their tasks, and their job responsibilities; and to see how we might better organize our tasks to meet persons' needs and the job responsibilities within the church structure.

This book is a beginning study of volunteerism. We will only touch the surface with some brief ideas and concepts needed for working with volunteers. We will be touching upon the following areas as they relate to the church and working with volunteers: (1) Theology; (2) Supervision and Volunteerism; (3) Motivation; (4) Adult Learning; and (5) Evaluation.

It is not the purpose of this book to provide all the answers on volunteers or to be all inclusive, but to—

• provide input in areas that are not fully covered in other resources, and
• present a *beginning step* or *handle* for workers with volunteers in the church setting.

You, as a worker with volunteers—a supervisor—must now reach out and continue your growth to become more effective in that role!

Our first step will be to define some of the roles of volunteers, volunteer leaders, and supervisors. The word "volunteer" can be confusing and, in some ways, misleading. We can talk about a volunteer from two perspectives. First, we can see a volunteer as merely a person who offers himself or herself without any obligation to do a certain job or to take on a certain responsibility. Second, we can view the word *from the perspective of the person* who is doing the job or assuming the responsibility without pay.

A helpful definition comes from Kenneth D. Blazier, director of the Department of Educational Planning Services for the American Baptist Churches in the U.S.A. Mr. Blazier uses the statement:

"Volunteer is a noun and not a verb!"

This means that the word "volunteer" refers to the person and not the act of volunteering. Throughout this book I will be writing from this perspective—that *the volunteer is the person who is serving and not the act of volunteering*. Therefore, to define "volunteer," we can say:

A volunteer is a person who serves
without any financial remuneration.

A second definition that we need to have concerns the term "volunteer leader." In many articles and books dealing with volunteerism, the words "volunteer" and "leader" are used together meaning that there are volunteers, but also there are volunteers who are leaders. It is my belief that within the church all positions filled by volunteers are leadership positions. Therefore, to say "volunteer leader" is unnecessary. When we refer to the volunteer, we are talking about a person who is serving in a leadership position. Leadership positions in the church can be so varied as to include the janitor, the members of the various boards and committees, chairpersons of the boards and committees, church-school workers, secretaries, youth workers, choir directors, officers in the women's and men's organizations, etc. The volunteer in the church is a person who has assumed some leadership by the very act of accepting a position or a job responsibility and who is fulfilling that function without pay!

There is one more term that we need to discuss and define and that is the position of "supervisor." Within the church we generally have not used the title or had a position called "supervisor." Many persons may feel that this title refers only to positions in the secular or business world and has no place in the church. But in actuality there are many persons in the church who are now serving in positions and are fulfilling roles that could be legitimately be called supervisory! A supervisor is really an enabler, one who helps volunteers do their job. In management terms we might say that a supervisor is:

The first line manager who works directly with persons to
make sure things get done!

It is the supervisor's job to get things accomplished, but this does not mean doing it by himself or herself. To be complete and accurate, a definition of a supervisor must say that he or she gets things accomplished *with* and *through* people! It is the supervisor's task to *guide* and to *help motivate* persons toward the common group objective or goal.

Keith Davis, writing in *Supervisory Management,* states:

> Essentially, the supervisors perform a supportive role for their people. They try to supply the psychological, technical, and economic support necessary to get the job done. By providing such support supervisors make the worker's job easier, more satisfying, and more effective.[1]

Why should we talk about supervision and supervisors within the church? Simply because there has been little proper help, guidance, and support (which comprise appropriate supervision) of volunteers. Most volunteers are left on their own, which many times causes feelings of lostness and confusion and a sense that there is an overwhelming job to be done. These feelings can lead to a lack of motivation in the individual volunteer. This condition may also lead to the job not getting done, not being done adequately, or the volunteer quitting his or her position.

Sometimes this lack of supervision comes from an improper understanding of the roles of supervision and administration. *Administration* is the short- and long-range planning, the development of policies, and the major decision making. *Supervision,* on the other hand, is the act of or responsibility for putting the administrative decisions and plans into practice and action!

To answer the question "Who is the supervisor? " we can say: He or she is the person who is directly related to the volunteers. The supervisor is the person who is involved in the building of the support system and the motivational climate that enable the volunteers to fulfill their functions. Within the church a supervisor can be:

- a pastor,
- a chairperson of a committee or board,
- a president of a club or organization,
- an adviser or sponsor,
- a church school superintendent,
- a leader of a group of teachers.

Anyone who is fulfilling a supportive function as he or she works with individual volunteers in the fulfillment of their responsibilities and duties is a supervisor! We are not talking in terms of a supervisor being a "boss" or an "authority"; the supervisor lends support and encouragment to the volunteer as he or she does the job assigned.

2
A Beginning Theology for Workers with Volunteers

It is my firm belief that within the Christian community we need some intentional thinking in regard to our relationships with God, with other persons, and with the church in which we serve. Intentionally thinking through these ideas and concepts will enable us to understand many of our own actions and feelings. Theology establishes a framework and a methodology for understanding who we are, what God is like, who the volunteers are as children of God, and an understanding of the structure in which we are to operate.

The term "theology" may scare you as it scares many persons. A picture comes to mind of an austere, intellectual, theoretical professor-theologian who, within the cloistered classroom, expounds theological concepts and ideas in words that the ordinary person does not begin to understand. In reality, theology should not be something that seems scary to you or other persons, for theology is the study of God and God's relationship with persons. It is something that we all do, but perhaps not in a formalized or systematic manner.

"Theology" comes from two Greek words: *theos*—meaning "deity" or "god," and *logos*—which means "a study of" or "a rational thought about." Therefore, "theology" simply means "a rational thought about God."

Theology, narrowly defined, is only concerned with the study of God; broadly defined, theology takes in the entire relationship of God and persons. Theology has as its scope all personhood and an individual's interrelationships with self, with God, and with other persons.

Following are some suggestions of a theology for persons who serve as supervisors of volunteers in the church. This theology is presented to stimulate the reader's thinking and study in his or her own personal theological development.

GOD

For those of us who work with volunteers, and for the volunteers themselves, a positive and alive relationship with God needs to be at the core of our theology. All actions and all relationships are built upon and extend from this core relationship with the living God!

How we perceive ourselves and others stems directly from our relationship with God. If we see God as alive and in the process of growth and change, we can enter into those situations of change and growth less fearfully and with better preparation. If we feel that God is involved, we can better enter into the unknown—those situations of risk, growth, and change—in an attitude of hope and faith!

On the other hand, if we view God as unmovable, critical, and unforgiving, we will be less likely to enter freely into those relationships and situations where we risk failure. We then will be less open with ourselves and with others and perhaps less motivated to action and service. In this situation other persons may be viewed not as co-workers and enablers, but as adversaries and opponents.

A positive and alive relationship with God needs to be at the core of a theology of volunteerism. This theology believes that—

- God is loving and caring;
- God is *the enabler* of persons;
- God forgives and forgets;
- God is the source of all creation, change, and creativity within the world and within persons;
- God is the source of the skills, abilities, and talents with which we have been entrusted as stewards;
- God is the source of all growth and life.

This positive and alive relationship with God can come only from a relationship and contact with God. It means that we need to relate to God through prayer, study, listening, Bible study, living, other individuals, and worship so that we can understand God's will for us.

A *positive* and *alive relationship with God* needs to be at the core of a theology of volunteerism!

PERSONS

A theology of volunteerism sees persons as alive, changing,

growing, with a variety of skills, abilities, and talents. This theology sees volunteers as persons and not things to be manipulated, as humans who are responsible for themselves and their decisions and actions. A theology for volunteerism takes seriously the following five points:

1. Persons are unique.

Each person is unique and different; each person has been planned especially by God. This means that persons will have different needs and concerns!

2. Persons are not "things."

Persons are not things that can be or should be manipulated and moved about like pawns on a chessboard. Persons are a part of the holy and therefore part of the living God.

3. Persons need to be responsible.

Persons must take responsibility for their own actions and decisions. They cannot pass off their actions and decisions by saying, "The devil made me do it!" In reality *WE* (each one of us) choose what we do for ourselves. We must see that persons are responsible for their actions and choices and therefore responsible for the consequences of those actions and decisions.

4. Persons need and want a sense of meaning to life and work.

Persons need to feel and know that what they are doing is meaningful and purposeful! Each person needs to know that he or she is special and important to God and to other persons. People need to know that their lives and actions are appreciated by others!

5. Persons have different abilities, talents, and skills.

The theology of volunteerism needs to see and believe that God has given each individual resources in terms of abilities, talents, and skills. In some persons those resources are readily visible; in others these skills, abilities, and talents are found far below the surface and must be uncovered, cultivated, and developed. Through growing experiences, study, and experiences of exploration—in trust—these resources can be discovered, unearthed, and used.

A theology for those who are workers with and supervisors of volunteers is one that will see and believe that—

- persons are good,
- persons are alive,
- persons are changeable,
- persons are responsible,
- persons are responsive,
- persons are active.

This theology stresses that volunteers (persons) are striving for wholeness, maturity, completion, fullness, growth, and self-actualization in their lives, and that serving as a volunteer is a means of achieving these goals.

THE CALL, THE CHURCH, AND SERVICE

A theology of volunteerism takes seriously the fact that God calls persons to service; he calls them not only to full-time Christian vocations, but also to all places of Christian service. The theology also takes seriously the place of the church as a very important place for volunteer Christian service.

All persons have been called to follow God! The call is presented in two major parts and directions. First, there is the call to follow God in belief. This is the act of commitment and dedication of one's life. Second, there is the call to follow God by going forth in service and discipleship.

Persons respond to God's call and serve God in a variety of ways, using a variety of God-given personal human resources. The *world* is one important place of serving God, but the *church* is another place where one can serve and is called to serve God. As far as this book is concerned, the church is the central place of voluntary service. The church does have a mission in the world, but here we will only be looking at the mission which the church has within itself. The voluntary work we are looking at is that which is involved within the church and its related outreach into the world.

The church is people in the service of God. The church is composed of more than just the professional clergy. It is made up of men and women, boys and girls, who feel called to serve God and, therefore, serve God in many meaningful volunteer positions of leadership within the organizational structure of the church.

The church is people in mission. The church is people sharing their Christian faith, persons involved in teaching, leading meetings, serving on committees and boards, singing in the choir, cleaning the floors, planning—persons who by their very life-style are expressing their faith in the living God.

The church is people who are together. The church is people who are studying, worshiping, crying, giving, laughing, struggling, praying, growing, working, and serving together.

The church is people who realize each is unique. The church is people who see that each person is an individual and therefore different, that each person brings something unique and special to God's ministry and service, and that each person therefore brings his or her own special talents and abilities to the community of faith.

The church is people who are different, one from another, but who are together in their commitment and belief that Jesus Christ is Lord!

JESUS AS A LIFE-STYLE MODEL

We can discuss a theology, but many times it is more helpful and meaningful to picture through an example what is being talked about or written about. It is my feeling that the best picture or example of a lived theological life-style model for working with volunteers is found in the person of Jesus. Through his life we can see and identify, with our own practical human eyes, this "theology come alive!"

1. Jesus had a relationship with God.

A relationship with God was the basis of the life and actions of Jesus. In the New Testament we find numerous instances in which Jesus is found in conversation-prayer with God. Through this relationship Jesus knew himself to be called and sent. Jesus knew that his whole life was involved in the service of God. He was to bring honor and glory to God. It was through this strong relationship with God that Jesus gained his direction, purpose, confidence, strength, hope, and authority for his ministry and for his living.

2. Jesus was person centered.

Jesus was willing to put persons above the task that he was involved in doing. Jesus was also willing to put persons above the laws of humankind. In Matthew 9:20-23 we see Jesus on a very important journey; yet he took time out to stop and share with a woman who needed his help.

His actions on behalf of persons led Jesus into many conflict situations, especially with the religious establishment and its leaders. They were goal, law, and task oriented, and not person oriented as Jesus was! For Jesus, persons were important and he gave them an important part of his life.

3. Jesus viewed persons as alive, active, and responsible.

Jesus viewed and treated persons not as things to be manipulated, but as unique and special beings. Jesus believed that persons were created as individuals by God and, as persons, could decide things for themselves. To Jesus, persons were responsible.

In Matthew 10:16-22 we can see an example of this part of Jesus' life-style theology at work. In this passage we find an encounter of Jesus with his disciples. We see that Jesus was very honest in describing the task and the life ahead for those who were to follow him. Jesus did not make it sound easy, nor did he try to paint a rosy picture of what was to happen. Jesus did not try to force the disciples to follow him. He made each disciple responsible for his own actions and decisions. We might even assume that there were other persons, called by Jesus, who chose not to follow him because of the cost involved.

Jesus viewed persons as active, alive, and responsible. A vital part of being active, alive, and responsible is change; Jesus believed that persons could change, and, in fact, he wanted persons to change in the directions of growth, maturity, and wholeness.

4.   Jesus was perceptive of persons' needs.

Jesus saw the inner needs of persons and spoke to those needs. He really listened to persons speak, both verbally and nonverbally. The rich young ruler was perceived, by Jesus, as one who was worshiping his wealth and therefore had allowed riches to become a block to his entry into the kingdom. The parable of the unforgiving servant (Matthew 18:21-35) was perhaps told to Peter because Jesus knew that Peter had not been as forgiving as he should and therefore needed to hear this message.

Jesus spoke to the needs of the individual. He did not evade the needs nor did he try to talk his way around them, but rather Jesus got directly to the personal need of the individual who was talking with him. Jesus could be perceptive of the needs of persons because he listened (verbally and nonverbally) to persons and because he opened himself and made himself available to them.

5.   Jesus respected persons.

The fifth point follows closely on the above point. Jesus was a good listener. He respected persons enough to allow them to share their own ideas and thoughts. I doubt that we can find any examples of Jesus' interrupting persons or trying to put words in their mouths. Jesus listened! He might have disagreed with what a person was saying, but he still respected the person enough to listen and to allow him or her to speak.

The incident, found in the fourth chapter of John, of Jesus and the Samaritan women is an excellent example of this aspect of Jesus' life-style. A close view of the interchange will reveal that Jesus did not become a preacher, but he listened to the woman as much as he spoke to her.[1] A quick look through the encounters of Jesus will show us that most of the time Jesus began the conversation with a question and waited until he had heard the person's response before he spoke again.

Jesus respected persons and their feelings and ideas. He did not always agree with what persons said, but he respected them enough to let them hold their views and speak their views.

6.   Jesus used a variety of teaching and leadership techniques.

In working with persons, Jesus did not fit into one leadership or teaching style, but he used a variety of methods and styles. Jesus changed his style, depending upon the situation and what he wanted to communicate. At times he preached; at other times he told stories, used illustrations, or raised questions to allow persons to answer for themselves; and still at other times Jesus set an example for action.

As we read of the various encounters of Jesus, we can note that much of the time he gave persons the responsibility for drawing conclusions and making decisions for their own personal lives. Jesus did not try to give all the answers, but he allowed persons to draw the learnings and understandings for themselves.

Jesus used a variety of leading and teaching methods and styles, depending upon the situation, the persons involved, and the message he wished to communicate.

7.   Jesus did not run from conflict situations.

Jesus did not perceive conflict or differences in a negative sense, but he used conflict in positive ways and as a meaningful part of the total learning experience.

Much of the ministry of Jesus evolved from conflict. Jesus did not run away from this, nor did he try to avoid it hoping that it would go away. In a positive and healthy manner Jesus handled each crisis situation as it arose.

In Mark 9:33-35 we read of a crisis developing within the group of disciples. The disciples were arguing about "who was the greatest." A bit further along (Mark 10:35-45) we find Jesus handling the request of James and John and read of the reactions of the other disciples. In each of these situations Jesus could have simply "let it ride" and not handled the problem. No doubt the problems would not have been resolved and would have continued to grow, perhaps into a truly big conflict situation. Perhaps this crisis/conflict could even have grown to the point of destroying the fellowship of the disciples.

Jesus did something about the problems. First, Jesus admitted that there was a conflict between the disciples. Second, he pinpointed the place of conflict. Third, Jesus dealt with the conflict at that point and did not let the problem grow or flourish.

8. Jesus delegated responsibility.

Jesus realized that he could not do all of the job or ministry by himself; so he delegated some of the responsibility to other people. Jesus called people to follow him, but almost in the same breath he sent them away saying, "Go and tell others!" Jesus called persons to follow, but part of the task of following was and is to take on some responsibility for ministry. This means that those who follow must go forth as ministers telling others the Good News!

Jesus realized that the task was big and that his time and energy had limits; so he involved others and gave them authority and responsibility to serve.

9. Jesus gave persons appreciation, praise, and encouragement.

We can see that Jesus understood the basic motivational and emotional needs of persons. Jesus realized that persons need to feel appreciated and cared for even if they are doing what is expected of them. Jesus gave persons the feeling of meaning and worth in their jobs.

In Matthew 16:18-19 we see Jesus expressing appreciation and praise to Peter for his confession of Jesus' identity. And in Matthew 26:6-13 we see Jesus affirming and appreciating the actions of a woman whose behavior the disciples could not understand.

Jesus lived and worked with persons, knowing that appreciation, praise, and encouragement help to establish the climate that can best facilitate motivation.

From the above nine points we can see a theology lived and alive. We can see that Jesus was not working with paid professionals, but that he was working with volunteers. The spirit Jesus presented, in his total life-style, is truly a theology for volunteerism and one that can be followed by each of us in our relationships with the volunteers with whom we work.

3
The Supervisor

A great deal of the volunteer's response, whether positive or negative, has to do with the help, direction, assistance, encouragement, and support that the volunteer receives. It is the supervisor, directly related to the volunteer, who provides the needed help, direction, assistance, encouragement, and support!

Supervision is more than a role! Supervision is more than a job!

Supervision is—
- an *enabling relationship* which helps persons get things done, gives guidance, and gives support to the volunteer;
- a *process,* as the supervisor relates to each volunteer as a unique person, having his or her personal needs, concerns, hopes, skills, and abilities;
- dealing with problems and conflicts as they arise;
- giving direction; and
- working with volunteers as they fulfill their job responsibilities.

A supervisor, then, is—
- an enabler of persons;
- a person who expects good work from the volunteers;
- a person who lets the volunteers do their own jobs;
- a person who can clearly give directions;
- a person who can see the importance in the volunteers' positions;
- a person who is helping each volunteer to find satisfaction and personal fulfillment in his or her service; and

- a person who is growing in the needed skills of interpersonal relationship, communication, group dynamics, planning, conflict management, listening, and faith sharing.

WHAT IS THE SUPERVISOR'S JOB?

The supervisor is a manager. A manager is one who works well with persons! According to many management experts, an effective supervisor as a manager fulfills five basic functions.

1. Planning

The first of the managerial functions is that of planning. Planning consists of determining what should be done in the future. It includes the establishment of goals, objectives, and procedures, and the making of plans to achieve those goals and objectives.

Planning is a process of *decision making*. Decision making consists of looking at various possibilities and of selecting the one or ones most practical and feasible to be followed.

Planning needs to be done at all levels. Planning needs to be done by the various boards and committees as well as by the church school, the trustees, or the head usher.

Unfortunately, planning is one of the areas in which many churches fail. Therefore, these churches proceed without direction or knowledge of what needs to be done. In reality—

Fuzzy goals = Fuzzy results
No goals = No results.

As workers with volunteers we need to know what we want to see accomplished. We need to plan. We need to have goals and a plan for achieving those goals.[1]

2. Organizing

Organizing means establishing necessary structures, divisions, departments, and positions to get the task done.

An important part of the organizing task is *delegation*. Delegation is assigning certain tasks and duties to persons, thus giving them jobs to perform. Theo Haimann and Raymond L. Hilgert write:

. . . delegation of authority is essential to the creation and operation of an organization. It is the process of delegation of authority that breathes life into the organization. *Delegation of authority* means the granting of enough power to subordinates so that they may perform within certain limits.[2]

Delegation follows the realization that supervisors have only a certain amount of time and energy and cannot do the job all by themselves. Perhaps supervisors fail at this point more than at many others. Nothing is more demoralizing or builds more negative motivation than having a job assignment but finding out that one's supervisor has already done the job.

Delegation does not mean that the supervisor forfeits responsibility or that the supervisor does not help the volunteer with the job. It means that the supervisor gives volunteers clearly defined responsibilities to fulfill and encourages and trusts them to fulfill those responsibilities.

3. Staffing

The third managerial task is that of selecting, recruiting, and training volunteers. In the section on motivational climate, chapters 4 and 5 of this book, there is considerable discussion of this significant task for the supervisor.

4. Directing

Directing is—

* the guiding,
* the teaching,
* the training, and
* the helping

of volunteers. Once a person is in a position, he or she should not be forgotten! Therefore, directing is the influencing and leading of a person in the fulfillment of assigned responsibilities.

Directing is important! All the best planning and organization will be useless unless the supervisor is willing to guide and direct the volunteers. Directing is a task that will take the major percentage of the supervisor's time. Chester R. Leighty makes a very true statement that I believe all supervisors should memorize. Leighty says, "Time spent in developing leadership is repaid not once, but many times over the years."[3] Directing *does not* mean always looking over a person's shoulder and telling him or her what to do or not to do. Directing means that the supervisor gives the volunteer attention when it is needed, checks periodically to see if progress is being made, and considers the personal feelings of the volunteer.

A supervisor who continually is pushing or checking is just as demoralizing as one who does the job for the volunteer or one who lets the volunteer function without support and direction. Studies have shown us that general supervision lends itself more to high production. These studies show as well, however, that though persons do not want close supervision, they still desire some genuine interest, concern, and direction from the supervisor.

Supervisors need to establish a rapport with the volunteers and thereby judge when and where they may need assistance or guidance in the performance of their duties.

5. Controlling

The last of the five managerial functions is controlling. *Controlling is the process of evaluation,* and we will look at evaluation in depth in chapter 6.

Basically, controlling is checking to see if the objectives that were established in the planning stage are being met. Controlling, then, relates to the planning function as it corrects the shortcomings or the deviations from the plan. Controlling is the continuing evaluation of the program and the volunteers.

THE VOLUNTEER SUPERVISOR

We must remember that the person who is serving as a supervisor in the church most often is doing so as a volunteer. It is important to know that the motivational climate to be discussed in chapters 4 and 5 of this book also is applicable to the volunteer supervisor.

A person who serves as a volunteer supervisor needs—

- a sense of calling to the job of supervisor,
- the proper recruitment and orientation to the job of supervisor,
- a specific job description and contract or agreement with lines of authority and responsibility clearly defined,
- a continued program of in-service training and skill development, and
- a periodic evaluation of his or her work.

Those persons serving as professional supervisors (pastors, associates, Christian education ministers, children's workers, etc.) must be very aware of the responsibilities they have toward the volunteer supervisor and his or her need for support, guidance, training, and encouragement.

THE TRAINING OF THE VOLUNTEER SUPERVISOR

The person who is a volunteer serving as a supervisor of volunteers needs training in some special areas of human relations and specific skills. As I stated above, supervision is a relationship. It is a relationship between persons. According to Reginald McDonough,

"An effective supervisor must relate to each person differently. He must treat every one according to his needs."[4] Therefore, the growing supervisor must be continually seeking to understand himself or herself and to understand other persons and their behavior.

Peter Drucker, an eminent professor of management, writes:

> Self-development of the effective executive is central to the development of the organization. . . . As executives work toward becoming effective, they raise the performance level of the whole organization.[5]

Though Drucker is writing about the secular executive, what he says applies to the volunteer supervisor in a voluntary organization such as the church. When leaders grow in their skills, the performance level of the organization is raised.

Some of the general areas for training that would be very appropriate for the volunteer supervisor are: understanding human behavior; understanding motivational dynamics; understanding group dynamics; use of conflict management; communication skills; planning skills; ability to discover persons' and volunteers' needs, skills, talents, and abilities; personnel management; and training for peer counseling. (Note: Appendix A is a resource that may be useful in helping identify the areas of training needed by the volunteer supervisor.)

STYLES OF LEADERSHIP AND SUPERVISION

How a supervisor manages or supervises is very important! The style of leadership used by the supervisor determines the climate of the organization and thereby has a great effect upon the motivation of individual workers. As we look at the position of the volunteer supervisor, it is essential that we also examine the various styles of leadership that may be expressed by individual supervisors or leaders.

In the last few years a great deal of research has been done in the area of leadership, the various leadership styles, and their effects upon the individual. These studies have produced a multitude of classifications of leadership styles and have led to the writing of many good resource books. In this section we will only present an introduction to leadership and some various possible styles of leadership.

1.   A Leadership Spectrum

Several writers feel that there is a spectrum of leadership styles for supervisors. Although these writers use different names for the styles, we have chosen five to include in this spectrum.

The first leadership style is that of *the Authoritarian*. On the far right of the spectrum is the authoritarian supervisor who *tells others what to do*. Little, if any, explanation is given for action and direction. The authoritarian supervisor simply announces his or her decisions. This style of leadership is very leader- or supervisor-centered. The authoritarian leader believes that he or she knows what is best for the volunteers.

The second leadership style is that of *the Persuader or Seller*. The persuader style of supervisor, much like the authoritarian, makes the decisions affecting the volunteers. The difference between this style and the authoritarian style is that rather than just telling what decisions have been made, this supervisor tries to persuade the volunteers that the decision was made in their best interests! This leadership style tries to sell the leader's decision to the volunteers!

The third leadership style is that of *the Tester*. This type of supervisor first identifies the problem, then suggests some possible solutions and decisions. But, prior to the final decision, he or she invites reaction and input from those persons who will have to implement the decision. The final decision is not yet made and is open for some modification from the volunteers.

The fourth leadership style is that of *the Participative Supervisor*. This supervisor works with the volunteers, assisting them by bringing information, data, and various alternative solutions. The decisions are made by the volunteers, with the participative supervisor being involved in the decision-making process. Here the supervisor acts as an enabler and guide, choosing to function as a participant at some points and leading at various other points.

The fifth leadership style is that of *the Laissez-Faire Supervisor*. At the far left end of the spectrum we find this supervisor. The laissez-faire supervisor is one who lets the volunteers do whatever they wish. The volunteers are really on their own and the supervisor does not give direction, advice, or help.

2.   Leadership Style Evaluation

It is realized that at different points and in different situations the supervisor will be called upon to play differing leadership roles. A problem may arise in which we allow one style to become the dominant way in which we relate to volunteers. The "authoritarian" or the "laissez-faire" supervisory style might be proper at some points, but not at all points! The volunteers whose supervisor is an "authoritarian" leader will feel that they really do not count. They will have a tendency toward a lack of "ownership" in their job responsibilities, which will lead to low motivation and a lack of commitment. On the other hand, if the supervisor is always practicing "laissez-faire" leadership, the volunteers will feel lost, confused, and overwhelmed by their responsibilities.

Much of the supervision we are now doing in the church is the "laissez-faire" style of leadership. Many volunteers are left on their own, "to sink or swim"! In reality there is no direction or supervision provided for most volunteers.

Is there then a style which is best for the volunteer supervisor to use when working with volunteers? It is my belief that the participative style of leadership and supervision best embodies the enabling, encouragement, and support that are needed by the volunteers. The "participative" leader or supervisor is one who works directly with individual volunteers, giving them understanding, care, and direction!

Each volunteer supervisor needs to evaluate his or her personal style of leadership or supervision to see if he or she is using one extreme or the other. The supervisor needs to identify places where there is need to change styles for better volunteer attitudes and production.

SUPERVISION AND THE CHURCH—A PROBLEM?

The supervisor plays an important part in the motivation and the fulfillment of the volunteers' job responsibilities. Volunteers therefore need and deserve to have the best supervision possible to assist them in their jobs. When volunteers take on responsibilities, they need a supervisor who will be responsible for them and give them a sense of direction and purpose.

Consequently, the volunteer supervisor is a very important person in the church, which depends upon volunteers and is completely voluntary in nature.

As was stated above, many volunteers have received little, if any, proper supervision within the church. There are perhaps many reasons for this, but I will identify four.

First, there has been a lack of proper supervision because of *an unclear definition of supervision and administration!*

Many supervisors have been involved in administration rather than in direct personal supervision of volunteers. There is always a certain amount of administrative work involved with supervision, but this *should not be* the major direction of the supervisor's job! The supervisor should not be involved in so much "administrative paper work" or in administrative decision making that he or she does not have enough time to work directly with the individual volunteers.

Supervisors need to have a *clear understanding* of their roles and responsibilities. Specific job descriptions are needed for the supervisory positions just as they are needed for all other volunteer positions. Such a job description should indicate the supervisor's responsibilities, to whom the supervisor is responsible, who is to be supervised, and how the supervision will be done. The job description needs also to specify what authority the supervisor has in the completion of his or her job and to whom the supervisor can turn for assistance in the completion of his or her task.

Second, there has been little supervision because *we have placed the wrong persons in supervisory positions!*

We, in the church, have sometimes placed persons in leadership positions not because they have the interests, abilities, skills, or talents of supervision, but for other reasons. Therefore, many times we have supervisors who are really incompetent in the task assigned to them. These persons may be good committee members, workers, or teachers, but they lack the needed supervisory interest or skills.

As we will see in the section dealing with motivation, we need to match an individual's abilities, skills, and interests with the abilities and skills needed for the volunteer positions. If this is true of the volunteer workers in general, it is also true for the volunteer supervisor!

Third, there has been little proper supervision *because of the church setting!*

We, in the church, have had difficulty seeing supervision as something other than a boss telling an employee what to do! We have had difficulty learning that *supervision* and *supervisor* are not just secular terms, but are needed to make any organization functional.

The idea that the supervisor is a "boss" has led church people to shy away from practicing supervision. In working with volunteers, the only power the supervisor has is in the area of advice, suggestion, and some direction. Even with just advice and suggestion, supervisors of volunteers in the church have been afraid of asking too much of volunteers or of "offending" them by making special comments and demands. There is the feeling that if the volunteer's supervisors give suggestions, advice or some direction, perhaps "someone" will get his or her feelings hurt and leave the volunteer position and perhaps even withdraw from the church. Therefore, volunteers have been allowed to continue without direction and support, sometimes even crying for help! Little face-to-face help, direction, or advice is given to the volunteers. And the help and advice that are given are many times the old "shotgun" approach in which a workshop or program is presented that tries to cover all bases and meet all participants' needs. This most often provides little support and direction and generally misses the mark of many individual volunteers' concerns.

A *fourth* problem with supervision in the church has to do with *a volunteer supervising volunteers.*

Sometimes volunteer supervisors feel inadequate and inferior to the volunteers they are supervising. A new chairperson may have members on his or her committee who have been serving in those positions for some length of time. A new church school superintendent may have teachers who have been teaching for many years and know all the "ins-and-outs" of teaching. In this type of situation the volunteer supervisor may feel that these "old hands" know more, are more capable, and do not need supervision. It may be true that a committee member or a teacher knows more than the supervisor, but that still does not remove the responsibility of supervision.

It is in situations like the above that I firmly believe the role of a *professional supervisor* is most important. A professional supervisor is the pastor, associate pastor, minister of Christian education, or another professional staff person. The professional supervisor is the person who needs to be working directly with volunteers serving in various supervisory positions. It is the task of the professional supervisor to—

- set an example of proper supervision;
- discover the needed skill development of the volunteer supervisors;
- develop an ongoing training program for the volunteer supervisors;
- provide the needed orientation to the job for the volunteer supervisors; and
- help to establish the climate of motivation and support for the volunteer supervisors.

It is the responsibility of the professional supervisor to assist the volunteer supervisors with their tasks and jobs. Part of the professional's job is to establish the groundwork that gives the volunteer supervisor a strong feeling of adequacy in his or her supervisory position and thus to help in diminishing the problems of a volunteer supervising volunteers.

I believe that we in the church need to spend a greater amount of time and resources working with persons who are presently serving as volunteer supervisors. We must remember that volunteer supervisors are the keystone to the complete organizational function and the motivational climate of volunteerism. This climate and organizational function will determine production level and whether or not the volunteers will continue to do their jobs! Therefore supervisors are the key to effective and meaningful work for volunteers.

4
Building a
Motivational Climate

Proper motivation is the real key in working with volunteers. This motivation is important at three stages of volunteerism in the church. First, proper motivation is important at the time the volunteers are recruited and accept the responsibility. Second, it is important as the volunteers fulfill their functions, that is, do their jobs. Third, proper motivation is important as the volunteers complete the jobs and are asked to continue in their positions.

WHAT IS MOTIVATION?

Motivation is one of those often used and frequently misused words that is difficult to define. According to *Webster's New Collegiate Dictionary,* to motivate is "to provide with a motive." A motive is that within the individual, rather than without, which incites him or her to action.

In this section we will define motivation, beyond just the dictionary definition, by exploring and describing two styles of approaches to motivation. We will then see how one of these styles relates directly to volunteerism and the fostering of motivation within volunteers.

1. Static or Outside Motivational Style

The first style has as its core the belief that persons are motivated from the outside. Those using this style believe that persons must be continually prodded or pushed from the outside by external forces and stimuli before they will do their jobs properly. This prodding and pushing is called, by many persons, "motivation." Persons are pushed to learn because of the reward of grades and the fear of failure and/ or punishment from the outside controlling party. Persons are pushed on their paid jobs by the reward of money and the fear of being fired by the boss.

In this style, the volunteer is seen as something like a "static mass" which needs to be formed and pushed into the proper shape. Holders of this concept feel that a volunteer will not do the job unless there is this outside force that will direct him or her or that will provide the needed stimulus to do a job.

Professor Peter F. Drucker, presenting Douglas McGregor's "Theory X," defines this style of motivation by writing:

> . . . the traditional approach to worker and working . . . assumes that people are lazy, dislike and shun work, have to be driven and need both carrot and stick. It assumes that most people are incapable of taking responsibility for themselves and have to be looked after.[1]

Another view of this first motivational style is provided in the *1962 Yearbook of The Association for Supervision and Curriculum Development,* in which the editors state:

> This static view of human motivation has been with us a long time. It tends to see the human organism as basically untrustworthy and certain to move in the "wrong" direction unless carefully supervised and controlled. Motivation in this view is a matter of controlling the external events to assure that the student (i.e., volunteer) will arrive at the prior and "proper" determined ends. It is basically a question of force, coercion, control, management direction, aimed at molding the child (i.e., volunteer) in "the way he should go."[2]

Though the writers of the above quote were talking about public education, this static view of motivation has also been the management style of the church in relationship with students as well as in working with volunteers. In the church we have tried to motivate from the outside by putting pressure and force on the individual volunteer. Many times this outward motivation has been by manipulation, by trying to produce guilt in order to get persons to accept positions, carry out the jobs, or continue serving.

In the church we have seen motivation as stimulus and response or direction and control. Therefore, many times, when one has asked the question "What can I do to motivate the volunteers?" the question really being asked is, "What is the correct control that I can use that will get the response and the results that I want from the volunteers?"

2.   Positive or Inner Motivational Style

The second motivational style stems from the belief that we really cannot motivate a person from the outside, but that a person is only motivated from within himself or herself.

Volunteers are then motivated by the things that they find meaningful and satisfying, the things that they feel (either consciously or unconsciously) are important. The inner needs and desires of the volunteers motivate them to action and service. The basic assumption of this second motivational style is that *persons motivate themselves.*

Volunteers, then, are motivated from personal needs and concerns. These needs will differ at varying times and in differing situations for each volunteer. The motivational needs which cause volunteers to assume leadership will not necessarily be the same needs that will motivate them to fulfill the job or to continue (be retained) in the position.

The psychologist Abraham Maslow has done a great deal of study in the area of individuals and their needs. Maslow feels that all persons have a dominant set of needs which motivate their behavior. Maslow also believes that only a person's unsatisfied needs are prime sources for motivation.

In his studies Dr. Maslow has identified five major groupings of needs, and he has arranged these five into a pyramidal system he calls a "Hierarchy of Needs." At the base of the pyramid are physiological needs, such as food, oxygen, and waste elimination; at the next level are safety needs, such as freedom from fear and the need for law and order; next up on the hierarchy are belonging and love needs—friendship, companionship, and needs for acceptance and affection; these are followed by esteem needs—self-respect, recognition by others, dignity, etc. At the top of the pyramid Maslow puts the need for self-actualization, which includes the desire to create, the desire for growth, and, in general, the realization of goals which allow the person to become what he or she wants to become. Dr. Maslow believes that a person must satisfy those needs at the bottom of the hierarchical pyramid before he or she can be concerned with those needs of a higher level. Once a need has been fulfilled, it no longer serves as a motivational factor for the individual. Maslow also emphasizes that a person will be at different levels of need in different situations. At work a person may be at the safety need, but in the church he or she may be at the point of esteem needs being met. Therefore, needs are not universally the same, but in each situation the individual volunteer's needs must be discovered.[3]

To help volunteers effectively, we must try to recognize and understand their own personal motivational needs. One of the best ways to identify and discover these needs is by taking the time to talk with and listen to each individual volunteer as he or she shares hopes, fears, concerns, and self-identity. Listen to how the volunteers feel about their job assignments and how they feel about fulfilling those particular jobs.

When a volunteer's needs are being met or when he or she believes that those needs will be met, then there will be motivation! Therefore, it is important that supervisors relate to each volunteer at the point or points of his or her personal needs and thus facilitate individual volunteer motivation.

Dr. Frederick Herzberg has identified factors which he believes are motivational factors for workers. These factors are: (1) a sense of achievement, (2) recognition for work done, (3) a feeling of importance and interest in the work itself, (4) an opportunity to take responsibility, and (5) an experience of growth and development on the job. Herzberg believes that, when these five factors are present, there will be a positive climate of motivation created within the volunteers to fulfill their job responsibilities.[4]

Both Maslow's and Herzberg's theories should be taken into consideration by supervisors of volunteers. They are both important and helpful in establishing the motivational climate that will enable volunteers in the fulfillment of their respective jobs.

MOTIVATIONAL CLIMATE

Because volunteers are motivated by their own needs, all of the outside pressures that we might use would really not cause them to be more committed or dedicated or motivated to do their jobs. In fact, outside pressure may cause the reverse to take place and lead the volunteers away from positive motivation. In working with volunteers, there needs to be the development of a *total climate* that will touch upon the inner needs of the volunteers and thus provide a motivational incentive to achievement and job fulfillment. This climate is called the "motivational climate."

Persons responsible for supervising volunteers need to work at building this total motivational climate during five stages of the church's relationship with volunteers. The five stages consist of: preservice, selection of the volunteer, recruitment of the volunteer, orientation of the volunteer, and fulfillment of job responsibilities by the volunteer.

Because of the importance of the motivational climate for volunteerism in the church, we will be looking at each area in some specific detail. It should be noted that there are no distinct lines dividing these five stages, and there will be some overlapping. The balance of this chapter will be devoted to the pre-service stage, and the remaining four stages will be discussed in the next chapter.

The establishment of the positive motivational climate begins before any person is asked to assume volunteer leadership. The pre-service stage is the process of—

- *informing* persons in the church about the various responsibilities and jobs, what volunteers are now doing, and what is expected of the various jobs;
- *developing criteria of leadership* through which the church determines just what types (qualities and skills) of persons are wanted for leadership within the church;
- *developing job descriptions and job contracts* or covenants for each volunteer position in the church;
- *developing a skill, interest, or human resource bank* whereby the resource potential of the church members will be identified;
- *planning ahead* to meet the needs of the church, making use of the needs and skills of the volunteers.

The first part of the pre-service stage is the development of an ongoing Personnel-Nominating Committee within the church. Most churches have a nominating committee, but it is a committee which usually only functions for a short period of time prior to the annual election of church officers. The Personnel-Nominating Committee is a key ingredient for the proper motivational climate. The Personnel-Nominating Committee needs to become a fully functioning committee that will operate throughout the entire year. It is a committee that should be elected or appointed and given the responsibility for the total personnel needs of the local church.

The Personnel-Nominating Committee needs to receive from the church the official responsibility to function in the following six areas for the development of pre-service motivation:

1. The Development of Criteria of Church Leadership

Most churches will accept anyone who is willing to be a leader. Many times persons without leadership skills or the needed qualities end up in key church leadership positions. But the church must take leadership seriously and must come to the realization that not all church members are qualified for all leadership positions. The Personnel-Nominating Committee needs to look at and decide what type of person is wanted and specifically who they are looking for to be a leader in their church.

Step #1—Brainstorm the Desired Leadership Qualities. The committee should spend some time brainstorming the answer to the question "What qualities do we want in a leader?" As the qualities are mentioned, they should be written on a large piece of newsprint for all committee members to see. Some of the qualities that might be developed are:

- dedicated Christian,
- open,
- creative,
- able to communicate with others,
- able to work with others,
- willing to grow,
- able to communicate a personal faith.

Step #2—Define the Terms. After brainstorming, the committee needs to take some time to define the terms written on the newsprint. In brainstorming, the committee was developing a potential list of desired leadership qualities; now the committee has to make sure that it has an agreement as to what each of the terms means. At this time the committee members may find some duplication of terms and may want to amend the listing.

Step #3—Prioritize Qualities. This step consists of taking the leadership qualities and placing them in an order of priority. First, have each committee member do this on an individual basis by numbering the list, with number 1 being the highest priority, number 2 the next priority, etc. Second, have members of the total committee share their prioritized lists. By having the members share their priority listings, you will get a good idea of the group priority listing. Add up the points on the individual lists to find the group totals. (Example: A number 1 priority will count 1 point; number 2 will count 2, etc. By adding up the number of points each quality receives, you will then have a prioritized listing of leadership qualities as seen by your committee. The item with the *smallest* number is seen as having the greatest priority.)

At this point the committee should agree that this list is the prioritized list of qualities needed for leadership coming from this committee. Revisions in the list may be necessary before final consensus is reached.

Step #4—Check Out Response from Committees, Officers, and Boards. The committees, officers, and boards of the church need to have opportunity for input, reaction, and evaluation of the listing of leadership qualities. Have these persons read over the prioritized list of leadership qualities. Ask for their response and their feedback.

After the list has been reviewed by the various persons, the Personnel-Nominating Committee may want to redo or rewrite the list of qualities. Perhaps some qualities will be added to or deleted from the listing after receiving the response from the committees.

Step #5—Secure the Approval of the Church. The "Criteria of Church Leadership" should be presented to the total church for its modification and approval. The approval of the criteria by the church or official board is important! When the criteria are approved, this says that the total church believes that leadership is important and that persons need to have some of these qualities before they can be asked to assume leadership in the church.

It is important that the church approves these criteria of leadership, for now they are the official means that the Personnel-Nominating Committee can use in the evaluation of possible volunteers. The approval also means that the church accepts the fact that all persons are not qualified for all leadership positions and responsibilities in the church.

2. The Development of Job Descriptions

The Personnel-Nominating Committee needs to develop specific job descriptions or job outlines for all positions of leadership within the church. Herbert Chruden writes of the importance of job descriptions by saying:

> A higher level of employee motivation is likely to be present where the duties and responsibilities of the individuals are understood, where lines of authority are clearly indicated, and where the objectives are clearly defined.[5]

Most church constitutions provide only a brief outline of the job responsibilities, and these are usually in very generalized terms. The Personnel-Nominating Committee needs to look at each position of service and develop job descriptions or outlines for each specific position. This means all positions: for committee members as well as chairpersons, church school teachers as well as the superintendent, secretaries as well as custodians. It has been shown that persons who are unclear of their job responsibilities will not be highly motivated to job completion or fulfillment.

Harriet H. Naylor gives us a good outline of what a job description for volunteers should contain. Mrs. Naylor writes:

> We ought to specify the objectives for the job, the time it will take, the limits of responsibility and the lines of accountability just as we do for employees. . . .

Such a job description becomes a valuable tool for recruiting, for selection and placement. . . . It should be possible for the individual volunteer to check himself against the description and see for himself what he needs to learn to supplement the qualifications he already has.[6]

As the committee develops job descriptions, it is important for them to discuss with and have the input from persons who are now serving in those positions. The committee would present a "working copy" of the job description to the person or group to receive a response.

Another approach would be to have each committee or person with job responsibilities write his or her own job description and then have the Personnel-Nominating Committee review, revise, and put the job descriptions into a uniform pattern. (See Appendix B for a sample job description.)

Some people would place the development of job descriptions under the stage of recruitment of volunteers. Job descriptions are an important tool of recruitment. However, I firmly believe that the proper place for their discussion is here in the pre-service stage because the development of job descriptions needs to be done prior to the contact for recruitment. Studies have shown that volunteers want to know what is expected of them. Volunteers want to have clear directions for their responsibilities from the beginning of service. They want to know up front the full picture which a proper job description can supply.

When the volunteers have a job description, they can then know what the expectations are and that there are no hidden expectations which will be thrown at them at a later time. The job description is a motivational tool which will help volunteers to enter into and fulfill their job responsibilities.

3. The Development of Job Contracts, Covenants, or Mutual Agreements

The job description is basically an outline of what is expected of the particular job. The Personnel-Nominating Committee should go one step further and develop job contracts or covenants which are mutual agreement forms. These contracts need to be developed for each volunteer position within the church.

Use of these contracts has motivational value in that they will spell out in very specific terms the purpose, goal, or objectives of the job; what is expected of the individual fulfilling the position; how long the volunteer is being asked to serve; and what the volunteer can expect from the church, committee, and supervisor in terms of support, supervision, training, and evaluation.

Appendix C is a sample job contract form. Note that it should be as specific as possible for the expectations and responsibilities both of the volunteers and of the church. Many studies of volunteerism have shown that volunteers deserve, desire, and need this type of written agreement which clearly spells out the job and the boundaries and expectations both of the volunteers and the organization.

There are certain risks involved which should be noted. As many individuals object to signing a church pledge card, so also many persons will have objections and fears in signing this type of form. At present, when individuals choose to fill volunteer positions, they do so feeling "It is a volunteer position and I can choose to go to the meeting, or miss the meeting, or to do or not do the job . . . it is only my volunteering." By signing a paper, they are signing something to which they will be held accountable. For some persons this will mean that the freedom of volunteering will be taken away and they will be somewhat forced to look at their position with a bit more seriousness.

Many of the fears and objections can be removed if the Personnel-Nominating Committee works with the individual volunteers involved. Interpretation and communication are key factors in removing fears and objections. The volunteers need to know the "why's" behind the job contracts-covenants. Also, volunteers should be involved with the input and evaluation of the job contracts-covenants. The volunteers need to see the contracts-covenants as something in which they too have an investment, something in which they have ownership, and therefore something not to be feared. The contract-covenant is meant to help the volunteers in their service and the church in its support and supervision of the volunteers.

4. The Development of a Skill, Interest, or Human Resource Bank

An effective means of motivation is matching the usable skills, interests, and abilities of the individual volunteers with the proper volunteer positions so that those skills, interests, and abilities will be used. The Personnel-Nominating Committee needs to have a resource bank to draw upon when it comes to finding the needed skills, abilities, and talents for specific volunteer positions. Following are some of the ways that information for the resource bank may be obtained.

First, a letter can be sent from the Personnel-Nominating Committee and/or the pastor. This letter would be sent to each church member and would explain the purpose of the resource bank and the importance of persons sharing their talents. Along with the letter would go a form that, when filled out, would show the various talents, interests, abilities, and specialized training of the person. This form should be filled out by each family member who is part of the church.

A local church can develop a form of its own, identifying those areas for which it is specifically looking. Appendix D has a sample form which may be duplicated as is or with revisions.

This form could possibly be returned during a special worship service built around a theme of talents and Christian service. The returning of the form could be an act of dedication and commitment of our God-given talents.

Second, you can have a visitation program. Churches may have many types of visitation programs. Visitation is done for membership and for stewardship commitment. Why not have a visitation program to discover the abilities, talents, skills, and special training of the church membership?

Persons would need to be trained for this type of visitation. There would be a standardized presentation for all callers. A possible format for the visit might be: a brief presentation about the purpose of the visit; discussion of the importance of volunteers in the church; discussion of the understanding of our abilities, talents, and skills as God-given gifts. The persons would then be asked to fill out the skill/interest form as an act of commitment.

Third, you can make use of personal knowledge. A discussion among the members of the Personnel-Nominating Committee, the pastor, teachers, and other leaders may yield much information about individuals who could be serving in leadership positions.

It is important to bring in as many other individuals as possible, because often one person's knowledge of individuals in the church will be limited. The more persons involved, the more names and information on prospective volunteers will be generated.

Do not trust your memory. Make sure that names and skills are written down for future referral.

Fourth, you can have a leadership fair. A leadership fair could be a fun experience for the whole church. A leadership fair is set up much like a mission fair with a variety of booths or tables, each dealing with some volunteer position in the church and the skills or interests needed to fulfill the position. Persons are free to wander about, stopping at the booths of their interest.

Some booth ideas are: (1) a booth offering personal assessment of talents, skills, gifts, and training; (2) a booth containing a questionnaire to help participants identify factors that have motivated them or would motivate them to service; (3) one having copies of job descriptions, job contracts-covenants, and resource aids for each committee, board, or leadership position. There should be a person at each table to answer questions and pinpoint possible volunteers.

The purpose of the leadership fair is to expose the entire church membership to their own skills, abilities, and talents and to point out the many positions in which persons may serve their church.[7]

Fifth, you can have a Commitment Sunday. A number of churches now have a Commitment Sunday for the financial program of the church. Why not have a Commitment Sunday for the commitment of our God-given and developed gifts, abilities, and talents?

The whole worship service could be geared around the commitment of skills, gifts, and abilities. The sermon would be based on the gifts we possess and the importance of using them. There could be litanies of dedication and a time to fill out the skill, abilities, talents, or interest forms. This would end with the dedication or commitment service as persons present these forms at the altar or worship center.

Once the information has been gathered by the Personnel-Nominating Committee, it should be compiled in the Human Resource Bank. A loose-leaf notebook with each page titled with a skill or an interest, listing those persons in the congregation with that particular skill or interest, could be easily used and updated! The Resource Bank might also contain a Personnel Section which would list persons and all their skills, talents, and special training. (See Appendix E.) When looking for a skill or talent, the Personnel-Nominating Committee might turn to the skill and talent section of the loose-leaf notebook. There the committee would find a list of possible volunteers. When there is a discussion of possible persons for volunteer positions, the committee turns to the person's name and there the members will find a listing of the individual's talents, interests, and specialized training.

A Human Resource Bank can be a very useful tool for the Personnel-Nominating Committee's work and will help with the motivation of volunteers by helping to match up the needed abilities and skills for the position with the right person for the job.

5. The Development of an Inventory of Needs

It is unfortunate that many times a church waits until the last minute to fill positions or even to realize that a position is open. The Personnel-Nominating Committee needs to work early in the church year and *plan ahead!* There are some positions that the committee knows will be open or up for election each year; so why wait until the last minute to find a person for those positions? The Personnel-Nominating Committee, working through the individual supervisors, needs to identify those positions that may become open in the course of a year.

Here are examples: A church school teacher has let it be known that he or she doesn't want to continue or would like to change classes. Or, a committee member is planning to move or has not been functioning well throughout the past year.

The Personnel-Nominating Committee needs to discuss: "What are the various positions that we will have to fill next year?" "What are the abilities and skills needed for those positions?" "Who are some of the potential persons to be placed in those positions?"

The Inventory of Needs should be kept on file and revised each year or as needed. Appendix F is a sample copy of a possible "Inventory of Leadership Needs" form.

The inventory form will help build the motivational climate as it matches up the right person with the right job.

6.   The Development of Publicity

Church members need to know what is going on within the various volunteer positions in the church. Much of what is known is often unofficial and misleading. We have all heard statements such as:

- "Deacons don't do anything except meet once a month and serve Communion."
- "Boy, if you let them talk you into teaching, you'll be stuck there for thirty years!"
- "It's only one hour a week!"
- "It's only one meeting a month!"

A means of publicity is needed to let the membership know what volunteers are doing and what is really expected in the various positions in the church. The church newsletter, words in morning worship services, or a special celebration of recognition are some of the possible ways of communicating the message.

Publicity (or communication) is an important function in building a motivational climate, as it will remove old stereotypes and present the real importance of volunteers in the life and ministry of the church. This may be done through the presentation of new ideas developed by the church, such as time limits on service, job descriptions, and contracts-covenants. Giving recognition to those persons now serving as volunteers will help overcome problems of recruitment and will help persons become interested in serving.

The pre-service stage is extremely important for the establishment of the groundwork for the total motivational climate. Here, in the pre-service stage, persons should begin to get the feel of leadership in the church. This "feel" can be either positive or negative. If positive, you will have a potential volunteer who will be motivated to serve. If the "feeling" is of a negative nature, the individual will, in all probability, not be motivated to join the ranks of the volunteer workers!

5
Sustaining a Motivational Climate

In the previous chapter we discussed the importance of laying the groundwork for a proper climate of motivation in the church that will facilitate the motivation of volunteer workers. In this chapter we will continue the discussion of the importance of this motivational climate as reflected in the selection, recruitment, orientation, and job fulfillment of the volunteers.

SELECTION OF VOLUNTEERS

The establishment of a climate that will lead to motivation continues into the second stage—the selection of the proper volunteer for the job!

The Personnel-Nominating Committee's job, at this point, is the matching of the job needs with the potential volunteer's interests, skills, and abilities. Unfortunately, many persons have been selected, elected, or appointed to church jobs only to fill the position. We must take seriously the selection process, and each potential volunteer should be considered in light of the job needs and his or her personal interests, skills, and abilities.

It is true that in many cases the church will take whomever they can get! In fact, sometimes persons are given leadership positions in the belief that if you give a person a job, that person will become active and involved in the life of the church. This is generally not true! Giving a person a position will not necessarily make the person more involved. In most cases such persons will continue in the same participation pattern they were in prior to taking the position.

The Personnel-Nominating Committee needs to discuss each position of leadership, the abilities needed, and possible persons who could fulfill those positions. Some churches have poor leaders continuing year after year because they do not explore any other possible leaders or they assume that the leader "would feel hurt" if not asked to continue. *All* volunteer leadership positions need to be discussed openly and frankly!

As you deal with each specific volunteer position, it would be helpful to have the supervisor of that position present and involved in the discussions. The supervisor may have a perspective on the job and the person being considered that may alleviate some possible personnel problems in the future. The supervisor may also indicate persons who should be considered as possible leaders, persons who should be considered for other leadership involvement, or persons with difficulties that may hamper leadership.

The *process of selection* is a very important part of the total motivational climate. All possible attempts should be made to match the volunteer with the proper position for volunteer service. Using the old adage about "round pegs and square holes," we can say:

> Round pegs will fit better in round holes (be motivated), whereas a round peg in a square hole will be less comfortable (and therefore be less motivated to service)!

RECRUITMENT OF THE VOLUNTEERS

The third stage in building a motivational climate among volunteers in the church is the whole recruitment process. Many times the church has recruited in a very haphazard, casual, and indifferent manner. We may talk to (or, should we say, catch) a person in the church hallway hurrying to or from worship. We may call the person on the phone and in the course of the conversation—usually right before we hang up and in a casual way—ask if the person is interested in serving. At times we try to recruit, not expecting the person to say "yes," and therefore we project an attitude of not really caring if they say "no." Or we may recruit with the use of negative statements:

- "You know that I'm on the Personnel Committee, and I have asked three persons already and they have said, 'No!' and I'm getting desperate. You're my last chance. You wouldn't like to be _____ next year, would you?"
- "You wouldn't be interested in being _____?"
- "I know you'll probably say 'no,' but I told the committee I would ask you to _____."

The process of recruitment needs to be taken very seriously! By using a negative manner of recruitment, we are indirectly saying, "The job really isn't important," and therefore also, "The volunteer isn't important either!"

In light of the seriousness of the recruitment process, I give the following general outline for recruitment.

1. Recruit well in advance of the needed time.

It is very discouraging to the motivational climate to start off running behind. When volunteers are recruited a few days before they are to begin service, they are put at a *big disadvantage!* Plan to recruit well in advance of the needed time. The "Inventory of Leadership Needs" (Appendix F) should be helpful in planning for filling positions which will be needed in the future.

2. Call and set up a time for a personal visit.

Recruitment, to be motivational and meaningful, should be done personally and not over the phone, in the hallway, or by letter. If at all possible, meet with the person in his or her home. This will provide a more relaxed atmosphere which helps the potential volunteer to feel more comfortable and at ease.

Going into the home also says to the potential volunteer that the position and recruitment are important enough that you will take some of your time for a recruitment visit.

3. Prepare for the visit.

Do not plan on talking "off the top of your head," but plan your presentation. As the recruiter, you must learn all you can about the position and the potential volunteer.

Take along the job description, the contract-covenant, and other related resources or program materials that may be helpful to the recruitee in making a decision. For example, to a prospective teacher you would want to take copies of the curriculum resources, a list of students, the number of the room and location, a list of supplies that are available, and a list of training events held in the past as well as those to be held in the future.

4. Take along someone who knows the job.

Take along either the supervisor or someone who is now serving in the position or a similar position. This person will be a good resource in answering questions and in giving additional background information and job expectations.

5.   Share with the potential volunteer the "Criteria of Church Leadership" developed by the church.

The potential volunteer may be thinking, "Why me? There are so many others who are better qualified for this position," or "I do not have the qualities to be a leader."

Share with the potential volunteer the skills, interests, abilities, or specialized training that he or she possesses that the Personnel-Nominating Committee believes to be important. Also share the qualities that the person possesses that match the "Criteria of Church Leadership."

6.   Listen.

Listen to the potential volunteer and encourage him or her to raise questions. If you are unable to answer some of the questions, tell the person that you will find out and give him or her the answers as soon as possible.

7.   Give the prospective volunteer a sense of calling.

Do not stress that the position is "easy" or "really not important," but stress the real importance of the job for the church, for the total ministry of the church, and for the recruit.

8.   Allow the potential volunteer time.

Do not push for an immediate "yes" or "no," but allow the person time to make up his or her mind, time to review the resources and his or her own personal time commitments.

Suggest a visit to the committee, group, or class so that the potential volunteer may get a better "feel" for what would be expected in the position.

9.   Set a time for another meeting.

Before you leave the prospective volunteer, set another time when you can get together to discuss other questions and allow the potential volunteer to respond. Usually a week or two will be enough time.

10.   Allow the prospective volunteer to say "no."

Allow the prospective volunteer the chance to say "no" without guilt or the fear of rejection. Do not force a "yes" answer, but encourage the person to keep open to the possibilities of future voluntary service.

If the potential volunteer feels that he or she is not qualified and needs additional training, suggest his or her participation in some training events that will be held during the coming year.

The recruitment process needs to be taken very seriously by the church. Recruitment is the first real contact with the potential volunteer, and, like a first impression, the recruitment process will either encourage and help or hamper and destroy the motivational climate.

ORIENTATION OF THE VOLUNTEER

In the fourth stage we find that the motivational climate is built through the orientation and introduction of the volunteer to the task and its responsibilities.

Many times volunteers, once recruited, are "thrown" into the job without any real knowledge of what is going to happen or what to expect. They find themselves confused, bewildered, and, in fact, lost with their responsibilities! When a volunteer is placed in a position without any orientation, he or she will be playing "catch up," and will find it extremely hard to be excited and motivated while struggling to keep one's head above water!

The process of orientation gives the volunteers some important handles so that they feel better prepared and more comfortable assuming leadership positions.

One of the possible methods of orientation is the use of *introductory training courses.* Many churches have a requirement that volunteers attend an introductory training course prior to assuming leadership. These courses are usually very general and cover a broad area that will need to be supplemented by more specific courses at a later time. Courses, such as "Being a Board Member," "Being a Deacon," and "Christian Education and Teaching," could be offered.

A second method of orientation could be *reviewing the job description and contract.* It may have been some weeks or months since the volunteers were recruited. A review of the job descriptions and job expectations might be extremely helpful. This review should be done by the volunteers' supervisor and should include the lines of supervision: to whom the volunteers are responsible and to whom the volunteers might turn for assistance.

A third method is *a review of the resources and the facilities.* The supervisor should personally take new volunteers around and show them the various resources available and where they are to be found. Perhaps checking to make sure the volunteers know how to operate various machines would be helpful. A quick review of the human resources available is also very important.

A fourth possible method of orientation is *attendance at a meeting*. A good orientation would be to encourage the volunteers to attend one of the meetings of the committee, board, group, or class prior to assuming leadership. This would be a good way of giving the volunteers a "feel" and a sense of belonging in the position and job.

A fifth method is *discussion of questions*. The volunteers may have questions that have come to their minds since recruitment. Time should be given for those questions to be raised and answered prior to leadership responsibilities being assumed.

Orientation is a way of enabling volunteers to feel good about their new responsibilities and about themselves in relationship to their new positions. Orientation of volunteers is an important step, for through the proper orientation the volunteers' motivational climate will be increased. If the volunteers feel good about their jobs at the beginning, this motivational climate will have a better chance of growing.

FULLFILLMENT OF THE JOB RESPONSIBILITY BY THE VOLUNTEERS

The motivational climate is fostered when volunteers know that they will be supported in their job responsibilities!

Often the church places persons in leadership positions and then forgets them. Harriet Naylor states: "Volunteers left to grow like weeds seldom get enough job satisfaction to sustain them."[1] What this means is that volunteers who do not get support and training, in most cases, will not do their jobs and will not be motivated to continue in their present positions, nor will they be motivated to assume other volunteer positions in the future. Unfortunately, this has been too true of the local church, and many good volunteers have been lost because of the lack of job satisfaction.

In this stage we will briefly identify seven possible areas of in-service or on-the-job fulfillment that will give a positive influence to the total motivational climate of the volunteers.

1.   Personal Growth

Volunteers need the feeling that what they are doing is helpful to others but also helpful for their own personal growth. What the volunteers are doing must have contact with who they are and also with their needs, plans, problems, and hopes. For their experience to be meaningful, volunteers need to feel that they are gaining needed information and a new skill that they will be able to use at several points in their lives.

In a recent study of work done by Patricia A. Renwick, Edward E. Lawler, and the staff of *Psychology Today,* the authors asked respondents to rank the most important aspect for their job satisfaction. The result was:

> It was the possibilities for self-growth that crowded the head of the list, including opportunities to develop their skills and abilities, to learn new things, and to accomplish something that would make them feel good about themselves.[2]

If this is true for the individual in the paid work force, how much more important it will be in the volunteer work force. The volunteers are motivated when they feel that they are growing and meeting personal needs. This is why it is extremely important to find a volunteer's personal needs and match those needs, as closely as possible, with the needs of the job and thus provide a place for personal growth.

When volunteers feel that they are growing, they will be more highly motivated to serve!

2.   Recognition and Appreciation

Volunteers need to feel that others appreciate and care about what they are doing. Volunteers need to know that their jobs are important and meaningful.

Frederick Herzberg, in his study of the motivation of workers, identifies *recognition* as a key factor in job motivation. Where there is proper recognition and appreciation, motivation will be high. But where recognition and appreciation are low or lacking altogether, motivation will be low and the volunteers will express dissatisfaction.

A quick look around at various successful volunteer organizations will show that these organizations give their volunteers recognition, appreciation, and rewards for doing a good job. Timothy Ragan and Norman Lambert remind us that "Unsuccessful volunteer organizations tend to assume (usually incorrectly) that their workers need no rewards or recognition because they receive all their satisfaction from task accomplishment."[3] This style of unsuccessful volunteer organizations has especially been true of the church's style of relationship with volunteers. The church has not given recognition, appreciation, or rewards because it has believed that volunteers' motivation was service to God and therefore they received satisfaction from the job or the service rendered.

Each church needs to find authentic and meaningful means of recognition for its volunteers. Some of the many possible ways in which volunteers can be recognized for their contributions are:

- appreciation dinners,
- awards, plaques, or certificates,
- recognition during times of worship,
- articles in church newsletters,
- articles in local public newspapers,
- personal words of appreciation and encouragement from supervisors and the pastor, and
- personal notes of thanks and encouragement from the volunteer's supervisor.

Recognition and *appreciation* are two key motivational factors in working with volunteers. When recognition and appreciation are present, the chances of positive motivation of the volunteers will be much greater. We all like to be appreciated and recognized and will perform when we are thus appreciated and recognized.

3. Training

In-service fulfillment should consist of a continuing training program for volunteers. This training needs to be in two areas: (1) general personal development and (2) development in areas of specific skills that are needed by the volunteers for the completion of their job responsibilities.

The importance of training is brought to us in this statement from Harriet Naylor. She writes: "Training can no longer be offered cafeteria style, but will need to be actively promoted as essential, if not required, for some jobs."[4] We, in the church, need to see that training is important and definitely needs to be a requirement for all volunteers!

First, we must *identify* those areas of personal training and skill development needed by the volunteers. Second, we need to *design* training experiences that will be *meaningful* for those volunteers who participate. A poor training experience can lose a volunteer to any other training experience, and also may discourage the volunteer from serving. Therefore a bad training event will be a double loss for the volunteer organization.

Some of the areas of general training needs that most volunteers need to develop are:

- communication skills,
- group dynamic skills,
- conflict utilization skills,

- goal setting skills, and
- planning skills.[5]

As we think of volunteer training, we should not think only of large-group training experiences. Perhaps a more meaningful training event would come from the development of small groups of volunteers working in an area of common interest. There can also be the development of one-to-one training, with the volunteers working with the supervisor or professional supervisor better to meet his or her personal training needs. Appendix G contains a sample outline of a one-to-one training program.

No matter what the model is for the training program, it should provide an experience in which the volunteers have an opportunity to explore new ideas, think through personal leadership needs, and continue to expand their understanding of personal leadership qualities.

Training gives the volunteers the handles they need to develop and grow. When training is being provided on a continuing basis, the volunteers will feel supported and encouraged and thus better motivated to fulfill their jobs.

4. Involvement in the Planning and Setting of Goals

The motivational climate is further developed when volunteers feel that they are part of an organization in which they have a voice in planning and setting of the direction of the organization. Evelyn Huber writes:

> A . . . source of motivation for members of churches or other voluntary organizations is a sense of ownership of the goals of the group. Motivation is greater when there is opportunity to make decisions and solve problems. Persons who feel their voices have been heard in setting objectives and planning programs are more willing to serve on boards, committees, or task forces, or to teach.[6]

Within the church we have been very guilty of giving volunteers jobs to do but not giving them any authority within the position. Decisions are still made by an older power elite. When this occurs, we wonder why people are not motivated or do not want to continue in positions and many times drop out of the church entirely.

Volunteers need to be involved in the planning and the decision-making process. No matter what the decision is, input should be obtained from as many persons involved as possible. Involvement will increase commitment on behalf of volunteers. Motivation will be higher when volunteers realize that they have been given some responsibility and input in the process of decision making.

5.   Team Development

An important part of the job fulfillment stage, as it builds the motivational climate, is the realization by the volunteers that they are members of a team! Often volunteers feel as if they are alone and doing the job by themselves. Even many volunteers on committees or boards feel isolated from other members. To have effective motivation, each local church needs to spend considerable time in the development of a sense of "teamness" within its volunteer organization.

Team development may be done by all the members of the teaching staff and the various boards and committees working separately. Or, it can be done by the whole volunteer staff sharing together and growing into a team.[7] Perhaps it is best to start building with the total team and, as an aspect of the process, group around functional teams, such as teachers, trustees, deacons, and other committees.

No matter how it is accomplished, it is important to have team development and a sense of "teamness" so that individual volunteers feel that they are not alone, but part of a greater volunteer team in the church. The motivational climate will then be strengthened!

6.   The Delegation of Responsibility

Motivation is fostered when the volunteers are allowed to fulfill the jobs assigned to them! We have touched on delegation in previous sections, but the importance of delegation cannot be overly stressed. It is delegation of responsibility that makes any organization truly functional.

When the volunteers assume the roles or jobs, the "authority" of their positions should be given to them. Sometimes, in the church especially, we give persons titles or roles, but they are not given the authority to do their jobs. The pastor, the chairperson, or the "older leader" may still be the person "in charge," making the decisions and setting the goals and directions. When this style of leadership occurs, the volunteers soon become discouraged. In this type of situation there is little motivation and the volunteer may finally say, "I really do not count!" This volunteer is lost for the fulfillment of this position and perhaps any further volunteer positions.

The volunteers need to be given the appropriate "authority" with their specific jobs as it is spelled out in their job descriptions. They should be encouraged to assume the assigned responsibilities.

When volunteers are free to operate in their jobs, they then feel trusted and the climate of motivation for them will be increased.

7. Evaluation

The final aspect of the job fulfillment stage is the evaluation of the volunteer's work. We will be dealing with evaluation in chapter 6; so here we will only briefly mention evaluation in light of the motivational climate.

Many persons shy away from any type of evaluation because they see it in a negative sense. Persons do not want to be evaluated out of a fear that they will hear that they are doing a bad job or that they have been doing something wrong!

But many recent studies of volunteerism show that volunteers want evaluation. These studies point out that the volunteers want to know how they are doing, especially in light of the job assigned to them.

Volunteers deserve proper and appropriate evaluation of their service. Each volunteer's job description should indicate that sometime during the year there will be an evaluation with the supervisor.

Perhaps a better term for evaluation is "feedback." This gives the feeling that you are communicating to the volunteers what has been seen and heard by you.

Evaluation leads to motivation when that evaluation is perceived as good and positive and is given not to destroy but for the personal growth and encouragement of the individual volunteer.

SUMMARY OF THE MOTIVATIONAL CLIMATE

Motivation is a real key in working with volunteers! If a proper motivational climate is established, there is a good likelihood that volunteers will fulfill their job responsibilities and will feel good about themselves and their jobs. When the volunteers do not feel that they are doing good jobs and when they are really uncertain as to what their jobs are or should be, then motivation will be low. Under these conditions there is also a good possibility that they will not fulfill the jobs assigned to them and that they will not assume other volunteer positions in the future.

Motivation is the key! As supervisors of volunteers and other individuals responsible for volunteers, we need to establish the proper motivational climate that will give each volunteer—

- support,
- encouragement,
- recognition,

- meaning in doing something worthwhile,
- feelings of growth as a person, and
- knowledge that he or she is appreciated and cared for by the church.

In this way we will insure the effective motivation of volunteers for job acceptance, job fulfillment, and future volunteer service.

6
Volunteers and Evaluation

We have previously discussed evaluation as an important function in the building of the motivational climate and as a means of helping and supporting the work of growing volunteers. In this section we will be discussing the evaluation process in more detail, what needs to be evaluated, criteria for evaluation, and a style that will help us in our evaluation of volunteers in the church's program.

Evaluation is important for the continued growth and development of both programs and persons. Without evaluation we have no means to discover areas of growth or places where growth is still desired and needed. Though evaluation is important and is desired by many volunteer workers, it is an activity in the church that we have often failed to practice and follow through on. There seems to be almost a fear of the evaluation process expressed by both the persons who should be doing the evaluation (supervisors) and from the persons who will be evaluated.

Many persons in supervisory positions do not like the idea of evaluating the activity and participation of other persons. Some comments that may sound familiar are: "Who am I to judge?"; "The person might get mad and leave the position or even the church!"

On the other hand, those of us who undergo the evaluation process often think of evaluation only in negative and judgmental terms! Many persons think of evaluation as only showing how poorly one is doing and not as a process of identifying places where persons are now doing a good job as well as helping pinpoint places where improvement and growth can occur. Therefore, many persons are fearful of evaluation because they do not think that they are doing a good job. They see others who they feel could do a much better job. These persons do not want to be evaluated because they do not want their feelings substantiated. They do not want to hear that they are doing a poor job!

Evaluation needs to be seen as something which is positive and not judgmental—a positive form of guidance and direction for the volunteers. Therefore, in working with volunteers we need to develop a firm belief that the evaluation process is something useful, helpful, and needed. As supervisors we need to help volunteers come to understand evaluation not as a judgment upon them as persons, but as an evaluation of what is done and as a learning experience to help persons improve job performance in our church's total ministry!

WHAT DO WE EVALUATE?

There are three general areas that need evaluation: (1) the work that is done by the boards and committees; (2) performance of the individual volunteer; and (3) relationship of the volunteer with the supervisor.

1.   Evaluation of the Functions of Committees and Boards

Some evaluation of the work or the program that has been done or is presently being done is necessary and important. This includes the functions of the committees or boards, classroom teaching, the leadership role, etc. Questions that should be dealt with are:

- How did the committee, board, or class function?
- What were the achievements of the committee, board, or class?
- Did the group reach its established goals?
- If the goal was not reached, why not?
- If the goal was reached, what were the key factors for successful attainment of the goal?
- Did each person feel that he or she had a meaningful part in the board, committee, or class?
- Did the members of the boards, committees, or class feel that they learned or grew from their participation and involvement?
- What could be done differently to make the group more effective?

2.   Self-Evaluation by the Volunteer

The second area for evaluation is that in which each volunteer evaluates his or her own participation and leadership function. The questions that will need to be raised are:

- Did I fulfill my job description?
- What were my goals or objectives and did I achieve them?
- Did I participate fully as a member of the board, committee, or class?
- Were there times that I should have spoken up and expressed my ideas and feelings, but did not?
- Were there times when I pushed my point too hard?
- Did I allow everyone his or her freedom and right to participate?
- In light of this evaluation what should I do differently next time?

3.   Evaluation of the Volunteer with the Supervisor

The third form of evaluation is that in which volunteers are evaluated and given feedback by their supervisors. The questions that are being raised and discussed at this level are:

- What did the job description say? How well did the volunteer fulfill the description?
- What are the volunteer's abilities and talents? Are they being used?
- In what areas could the quality of the volunteer's work improve?
- What are the volunteer's strong points?
- What are the volunteer's weaknesses?
- What is the volunteer's attitude toward the job?
- What specific recommendations or suggestions does the supervisor have for the volunteer's further development, growth, and training?

CRITERIA FOR EVALUATION

"Criteria for Evaluation" are found in the following six areas:

1.   The Established Goals and Objectives

Evaluation begins with the planning process and the establishment of goals and objectives. The better the job done in the planning stage, the easier the evaluation process will be!

Many times volunteers feel that evaluation is something that is being imposed upon them. They feel that someone else has decided what is going to be evaluated and then tells the individual volunteers. It is difficult to be motivated and to work toward goals that you do not accept or fully understand. Volunteers need to have a part in the planning and the establishment of the goals and objectives that they will be asked to carry out in their respective positions. Ted W.

Engstrom and Edward R. Dayton speak to this point as they write: "Good goals are my goals, and bad goals are your goals, is a fact of life. We feel most responsible for those things that we have had a part in generating." [1] Volunteers need to be brought into the earliest part of the planning process. Their input should be actively sought and their ideas seriously considered. This does not mean coming to the volunteer staff, committee, or board to "rubber stamp" decisions made on a different level. Not does it mean that after a volunteer speaks, the supervisor says something like, "Now that you have all had your say, this is the way we are going to do it!"

One of the reasons volunteers need to be involved in the planning of goals and objectives is the idea of *ownership!* When volunteers have some input, they will feel some ownership and personal responsibility for the goals and objectives because they have helped to develop them. When it comes to evaluation of progress in light of the goals and objectives, volunteers will be evaluating *their own* goals and objectives if they feel a sense of ownership about them. Volunteers need to be involved in the planning of goals and objectives and thereby will be more open to the whole process of evaluation in light of the established goals and objectives.

We must make a special note. Involvement of volunteers in the planning process does not eliminate the supervisor's responsibility for planning. The supervisor is still responsible, but has opened the door for input, ideas, and suggestions from the volunteers involved in carrying out the established goals and objectives. This process means that there will not always be agreement between the volunteers and the supervisors. The process and involvement are essential so that volunteers may know and feel that they are important enough to have had some real input into the planning of their own jobs.

2. Job Descriptions

Job descriptions establish a standard by which performance can be evaluated. Reviewing the job description will help the volunteers and the supervisors identify areas of fulfillment or places of needed improvement. Performance is set against the standards established by the job description.

With a written job description, both volunteers and supervisors know from the beginning what are the specific expectations for the particular position. This is one of the important reasons for having written job descriptions rather than nebulous expectations in the minds of supervisors and others. When the job description is not in writing, the volunteers may have one expectation and the supervisor or other administrator a completely different expectation for the position. When it comes to evaluation, the volunteer may believe that he or she is doing exactly what is expected, but the supervisor will see the situation differently if his or her expectations vary.

Written job descriptions are a must for the proper evaluation of the volunteer's job! By reading the job description and putting the volunteer's performance alongside it, one can quickly answer the question "In what areas were expectations achieved and in what areas were they not achieved?"

3. Job Contracts, Covenants, Agreements

Job contracts, covenants, or agreements are another point where job standards are established and can be compared and evaluated with the performance of the volunteers.

Review the job contract, covenant, or agreement, asking the following questions:

- Did the church fulfill its part? If not, why not?
- What could the church do to improve its support system?
- Did the supervisor fulfill his or her part? In what ways was the supervisor effective and supportive? In what ways was the supervisor ineffective in helping, supporting, or encouraging? If the supervisor did not do his or her job, why not?
- In what areas did the volunteer achieve or fulfill his or her agreement? In what areas does the volunteer need to work at improving in the next year or term?

It is important to note again that the involvement of volunteers in the development of the contracts, covenants, or agreements is a key to evaluation. If volunteers do not have input, they may view the contracts as something that is being put upon them or imposed from the outside. In this case the contracts are then someone else's and not really the volunteers' agreements.

4. Personal Observation by the Supervisor

An important criterion for evaluation is the actual observation by the supervisor of the functioning of the volunteers. Watching volunteers in service is the only real way of discovering how the volunteers are functioning!

In some situations (i.e., in boards, committees, and groups) the supervisor will be working directly with the volunteers and will have the opportunity to observe them as they function. In other situations (i.e., for teachers, youth workers, and small group leaders) the supervisors will have little or no knowledge of a particular volunteer's activity or performance. Under this condition the supervisor will have a difficult time with the evaluation of the volunteer's performance or in making recommendations for future training, skill development, or changes in the volunteer's style. Therefore, the supervisor will have to make a point to set up observation times so the volunteer can be observed in actual service.

Personal observation by the supervisors is really a necessity for proper evaluation! To be most helpful, a supervisor should plan on observing volunteers two or three times each year. Following each observation, the supervisor should give feedback as to what he or she saw and make recommendations for possible action, skill development, areas of growth, and change. At the end of the year the supervisor could then evaluate the progress of the volunteer from firsthand experience.

Personal observation is important in the whole evaluation process!

5. Personal Growth

Volunteers want to feel that what they are doing is important for others and that it is important for their own personal growth. Volunteers need to look at and evaluate their own personal growth and their feelings about self in relationship to their responsibilities.

Volunteers need a sense of personal growth. Each volunteer needs to evaluate himself or herself and his or her own perceptions of growth and development. The establishment of "growth goals" by each volunteer would be most helpful for the volunteer's personal growth and for the evaluation of that growth. Growth goals are statements of each volunteer which spell out those areas in which he or she wishes to grow or develop during a specific period of time.

6. Personal Feelings

What are the volunteers' feelings about their involvement and job responsibilities? Do the volunteers have accurate or inaccurate perceptions about their job responsibilities and their fulfillment? Two examples may help us to identify what is meant by personal feelings as a criterion for evaluation.

First: a teacher feels that this past year was a complete waste! He or she perceives that nothing was accomplished and that the participants really did not enjoy the year or learn anything. This perception of the teacher should be checked out with the students and others with whom the volunteer works. Input from the participants will either verify the teacher's perceptions or point out the inaccuracy of the teacher's belief. Perhaps the pupils will say that this was one of the best learning experiences which they have ever had!

A second example is of a volunteer who believes that his or her participation on a committee has been excellent: "The committee couldn't have done it without me!" This too needs to be checked out and evaluated as to accuracy. One of the best ways to evaluate committee work and an individual's participation is to have the entire committee evaluate the committee's functioning and each committee member's functioning. Important questions to ask include: "Who were the most helpful committee members?" "What were some of the problems within the committee?" "Should someone speak more or less? Who?" "Who raised the important questions?" "Who kept the committee heading toward the goal?" "Did you feel that you had a meaningful part in the workings of this group?" "Who was the real leader of the group?"

A system of feedback like the above would be helpful to a person in seeing if he or she should be talking less and working more. It could also point out that a volunteer should be speaking up more within the committee as other members respond, saying something like, "I wish that _____ would speak up more. Each time _____ has spoken, it has been meaningful and very helpful!"

Personal feelings are an important means of evaluation, but these feelings must be checked out as to the accuracy or inaccuracy of perception in relationship to the perceptions of others. Personal feelings are important, but sometimes they can lead us and others in false directions.

MODELING EVALUATION

Where do we begin in developing positive attitudes and approaches to evaluation for volunteers? One way we can begin is by trying to convince the volunteers that it is good for them. This, I think, would sound something like "What we are saying is for your own good, your growth, and learning!" But this approach may be taken by volunteers much as a child responds to parents who are preparing to spank him or her and who say, "This is going to hurt me more than it is going to hurt you!" The child really does not believe those words and neither would the volunteers!

I firmly believe that before volunteers will develop a positive attitude and approach to evaluation, we as supervisors, volunteer or professional, need to open ourselves to and participate openly in the evaluation process!

Supervisors need to begin by *modeling* the process of evaluation.

They need to be the first to enter the evaluation process. We who are supervisors must raise questions to generate feedback and evaluation of ourselves and our tasks. Questions such as the following need to be raised and asked:

- How am I doing as a supervisor?
- In what areas am I falling down in my job?
- In what areas am I doing my job well?
- In what ways have I been helpful to each person I supervise?
- Have I hindered anyone in his or her work?
- In what areas should I give more support or direction?
- In relation to the requirements of my job description, how am I doing?
- What changes should I make in my role as a supervisor?

It is true that at the beginning we should be prepared to receive a few strongly negative comments and, in fact, some hostile comments may be received. But we must model the appropriate responses that we desire volunteers to learn and use. The response we need to model is one that is nondefensive, open, listening, honest, and responsible. We are not asking to be walked over, but we are allowing persons to respond to how we are fulfilling our job responsibilities. Therefore, we must learn to separate job responsibilities and personality. We are being evaluated as workers and not as persons.

It may take time for volunteers to learn this style of evaluation fully, but we as supervisors need to continue to be open in our modeling of the style of evaluation we feel to be mature and healthy.

Beyond just opening ourselves up for evaluation, we supervisors need also to model the fact that we evaluate ourselves and our job responsibilities. We need to *demonstrate* that as supervisors we raise questions within ourselves regarding our functioning and performance. We need to be honest and share with the volunteers some of our inner-evaluation processes. Some examples of what we might share are:

- As I was looking at my job description, I realized that there is a large part of my job that I am presently not doing and must assume leadership in.
- I feel that I'm doing a good job in these areas: . . .
- I have come to the conclusion that I need more training, especially in communication skills.
- I am concerned about my personal relationship with you and whether I am really helping you with your task.

We who are serving as supervisors need to share our own personal evaluation process with the volunteers we supervise. We need to model the evaluation style and the positive attitudes and approach that we are asking volunteers to develop toward the process of evaluation. We need to be models of the behavior we wish volunteers to express!

Evaluation is really an important area in working with volunteers! The evaluation process is important, for it helps volunteers to determine whether or not they are doing their jobs. It can point out those places where changes and adjustments are needed for the volunteers' service.

Evaluation needs to be positive, nonjudgmental, geared to the job, helpful, practical, meaningful to the volunteers, and also needs to lead to some positive steps of change, growth, or support! Without evaluation, volunteers do not know if their personal and job goals are being met or why at times they seem not to be achieving very much. Evaluation gives volunteers a sense of direction and movement and a means to judge that direction and movement.

LOVE IS THE KEY

Whatever route is taken for evaluation, it must be taken in the *spirit of love!* When a supervisor says, "You are doing a great job," this is a statement of love. When a supervisor shares with a volunteer that he or she could be doing a better job, it is with the real belief that the volunteer can do a better job and is capable of change! When a supervisor says to the volunteer, "You are not cut out to handle this type of job," it is intended to show that the volunteer has other areas of possible service, to affirm the volunteer as a person, and to recognize other abilities and talents of the volunteer.

Love is truly the key for evaluation! The church, the community of believers, the fellowship of Christ, is based on *love*. Therefore, evaluation of oneself, another, or the group must be *given* and *taken* in the *spirit of this love. Love is the key!*

7
Volunteers as Learners

Most persons serving as volunteers in the church are adults. For those of us who are working with volunteers, trying to supervise them and to help them in their work, it becomes important to have some understanding of how adults learn. A supervisor is an individual who is trying to support and enable the volunteer to fulfill his or her job. One important means of support is to assist the volunteer in learning new skills, developing abilities, and appropriating these into his or her life and job function.

Therefore, a supervisor is an educational enabler, helping the volunteer to identify needed areas for growth and development and assisting the volunteer through an appropriate training program to grow in those needed areas! This is why it is important for us as supervisors to have some understanding of how adults learn. With this understanding we can better enable the growth and the development of the volunteer.

This chapter will not cover all the possible information on adult learning, but will only serve as an introduction to adult education. It is again hoped that the reader will continue to search out and expand these beginning ideas!

ADULTS DO LEARN!

We begin with the understanding that *adults do learn!* The old saying "You can't teach an old dog new tricks!" *is not true.* In fact, some studies have shown that adults learn better than young people. A look at the number of adults attending evening classes in local high schools and colleges shows that adults are interested in learning. Harriet Naylor points out:

> As adults, we take a little more time to learn, but we learn more thoroughly than children. Once we do decide to learn, we really concentrate hard because we plan to use the knowledge in the foreseeable future.[1]

Adults can and do learn, especially in areas that they feel are important, areas in which they have a need to learn, or areas from which they know they will be using information.

A difficulty in adult learning is often the *attitude* that the adult brings to the learning situation. Many adults will have feelings about learning and educational experiences which are very negative. This may mean that because of bad experiences some adults may need to unlearn some ideas about learning and education. Roy Ryan writes:

> One of the problems facing adult educators, in the church, is the task of helping adults unlearn poor attitudes, inadequate concepts of the faith, and established life patterns which may not project a positive Christian life-style.[2]

Therefore, adult education is basically a *process of change.* It is helping adults undo past experiences of education (negative ones) and develop a positive outlook or approach to education and learning.

LEARNING MUST MAKE SENSE

A second factor in adult learning is that *what adult volunteers are expected to learn must make sense to them as learners!* Adults learn when they can see the relationship between the learning event or experience and their needs in life.

Adult volunteer-learners need a real sense of and belief in the relevancy of the learning experience for their life, tasks, and job responsibilities. This means that many of our leaders' meetings, in which we sit and "chew the fat," will be meaningless and really negative experiences for many adult learners. Meetings in which little is done and training events that do not meet the volunteers' needs are really factors of demotivation. A training experience must meet the personal needs of adult participants and learners.

Most adults are motivated to learn and to participate in learning events because of very practical reasons! Most adults are motivated when they can see that they will be helped with their jobs or that the learning experience will speak to one of their personal needs!

For those persons who plan learning events, it should be noted that adults thus motivated will not withstand a lot of unnecessary "stuff."

They want to learn and they want the learning experience to be directed toward a specific goal. The adult volunteers will lose interest and become "nonparticipants" if the learning environment is too nondirected or if too many nonproductive things are taking place (i.e., starting late, off-the-subject talk, too much joking, etc.).

Adults come to learning events out of free will. Many of them have worked all day and are tired, and their energy level may be low. Therefore, they are selective about those things in which they choose to participate and to which they commit themselves.

What adults are expected to learn must make sense to them and must be done in an environment that also makes sense and is meaningful and productive. They must feel that their time is well spent and not wasted!

VOLUNTEERS NEED AN ENVIRONMENT OF SECURITY, TRUST, ACCEPTANCE, AND LOVE

The third factor in adult education or adult learning is that adults learn best in an environment that will allow them to overcome some of their past experiences and feelings about themselves and education. The environment that can best facilitate learning is one in which the learners will feel security, trust, acceptance, and love from the leaders as well as from other participants!

The *risk factor* in learning, for adults, is much greater than it is for children and young people. Adults enter into the learning situations with certain fears. Some of these are fears of failure, of the new and different, of what others might think of them, of lacking "proper" education, and of having "wrong" ideas or concepts or believing differently from others in the group.

Adults also enter into learning situations with built-in defenses from past learning events in which they have had "poor" experiences (i.e., put-downs, ridicule, being laughed at, being told they were wrong, etc.). Therefore, they have put up a defense and may not risk involvement and sharing again.

The first task for the supervisor or trainer of volunteers is to *reduce the feeling of—*

- tension,
- self-consciousness,
- fear, and
- intimidation

that the learners may bring into the learning situation! One of the practical ways to reduce fears is through some initial and continued *group-building experiences.* Group-building experiences can assist the adults to relate to one another, not as strangers or individuals to be feared, but as co-workers. When persons do things together, when they have common experiences, and when they start to share and talk together, the walls of self-consciousness and fear of the unknown become a bit lower!

To some persons group-building experiences seem "childlike," "silly," "stupid," and/or a "game" without reason. A group-building experience can be all of the above, but it *does* have a purpose. For it is through this type of experience that adults can laugh at themselves and with one another and thus reach a new plane of shared relationships. Group-building experiences provide *equalizing experiences* that will help reduce the bad feelings brought by many adults into learning situations.

Remember that for adults entering into learning situations the risk factor is very high. Many adults will feel threatened that they do not know everything or fear that they will make mistakes. Adult learners need the environment of trust, security, acceptance, and love that will allow them to lower the walls of protection and then to risk, so that learning might take place. Adults need to feel and know that it is all right for them to be who they are. Group-building experiences are one place and method of helping adult volunteer learners establish the best climate for learning.

VOLUNTEERS LEARN BEST WHEN THEY HAVE SOME RESPONSIBILITY

The final factor in adult education that we will discuss is that adults learn best in an environment where they have some responsibility. Adults need to know that they have had some part or some input into the learning situation. Adults many times know their wants and needs and, therefore, need to participate in the planning and direction of their personal learning experiences or events.

Adult volunteer-learners also need to have some avenue of feedback or evaluation following training events or learning experiences. They need a sense of achievement and progress. If the learners have been involved in the planning and the goal setting (have at least given input as to their needs, ideas, and concerns), then they will have some personal criteria for the evaluation of their progress.

Evaluation is a "two-way street." There is not only the evaluation of the "learning," but there is also evaluation from the volunteers of the learning *event* or *experience.* Such evaluation will help give the volunteers more of a sense of ownership and input into the planning of their personal growth experiences. This evaluation will be helpful also to the event leadership. Through evaluation the leaders will see where they have enabled learning or growth to occur or where they have missed the mark. This input from the participants is important for the planning of future training experiences and in the growth of the individual trainer or leader. (For a sample "Workshop Evaluation Form," see Appendix H.)

Although we have dealt with evaluation in a previous chapter, there is one more point to be mentioned here. Evaluation needs to serve as a tool for the adult volunteer's future growth or learning. Evaluation of the degree of learning and of the learning experiences leads volunteer learners and their leaders back to the initial step— *planning*. It is through evaluation that the volunteer learners identify areas of growth, needs for continual learning, and areas in which they want more knowledge or skills.

Evaluation, then, helps volunteers to assume responsibility for their real learnings (what they really got out of the experience) and aids in establishing a direction for future training and learning experiences.

SUMMARY

For those of us who are involved as supervisors and trainers of adult volunteers, it is important and necessary that we have some basic understanding of adults and of adults as learners. This understanding will assist us in the planning and the leading of meaningful training and educational events for adult volunteers.

Adults do learn and are willing to learn when it makes sense to them; when training is provided in an environment of trust, acceptance, and love; and when they sense some responsibility in the planning and the evaluation of their learning experiences.

As stated at the beginning of this section, this is only an introduction to adult education and adult learning. It is hoped that the reader will continue his or her search and study of adult education and adult learning.

Notes

Chapter 1

[1] Keith Davis, "The Supervisory Role." Reproduced by permission from *The Supervisory Management: Tools and Techniques*, ed. M. Gene Newport, copyright © 1976, West Publishing Company. All rights reserved.

Chapter 2

[1] See Masumi Toyotome, "Love Is Listening . . ." in *Going Public with One's Faith*, edited by R. James Ogden (Valley Forge: Judson Press, 1975), pp. 23-37.

Chapter 3

[1] For more information on planning, see: Kenneth D. Blazier and Evelyn M. Huber, *Planning Christian Education in Your Church* (Valley Forge: Judson Press, 1974) and Richard R. Broholm, *Strategic Planning for Church Organizations* (Valley Forge: Judson Press, 1969).

[2] Theo Haimann and Raymond L. Hilgert, *Supervision: Concepts and Practices of Management* (Cincinnati: South-Western Publishing Co., 1977), p. 38.

[3] Chester R. Leighty, *People Working Together* (New York: United Association, 1960), p. 16.

[4] Reginald M. McDonough, *Working with Volunteer Leaders in the Church* (Nashville: Broadman Press, 1976), p. 131. All rights reserved. Used by permission.

[5] Peter F. Drucker, *The Effective Executive* (New York: Harper & Row, Publishers, 1966). p. 170

Chapter 4

[1] Peter F. Drucker, *Management: Tasks—Responsibilities—Practices* (New York: Harper & Row, Publishers, 1973), pp. 231-232. Douglas

McGregor presents this theory in *The Human Side of Enterprise* (New York: McGraw-Hill, 1960).

[2] Arthur W. Combs, *Perceiving, Behaving, Becoming* (Washington, D.C.: Association for Supervision and Curriculum Development, NEA, 1962), p. 85.

[3] A. H. Maslow, *Motivation and Personality*, 2nd ed. (New York: Harper & Row, Publishers, 1970), pp. 35-46.

[4] Frederick Herzberg, *Work and the Nature of Man* (Cleveland: World Publishing Co., 1966), pp. 72-74.

[5] Herbert J. Chruden and Arthur W. Sherman, Jr., *Personnel Management* (Cincinnati: South-Western Publishing Co., 1963), p. 304.

[6] Harriet H. Naylor, *Volunteers Today: Finding, Training and Working with Them* (Dryden, N.Y.: Dryden Associates, 1973), p. 81.

[7] For more information on a leadership fair see: Unit #6 of the *Church Officer Development, Continuing Education Curriculum*, "Recruiting and Utilizing the Abilities of Church Leaders" (Philadelphia: The Geneva Press, imprint of Westminster Press, 1971).

Chapter 5

[1] Harriet H. Naylor, *Volunteers Today: Finding, Training and Working with Them* (Dryden, N.Y.: Dryden Associates, 1973), p. 16.

[2] Patricia A. Renwick and Edward E. Lawler, "What You Really Want from Your Job," *Psychology Today* (May, 1978), pp 56-57. Reprinted from *Psychology Today* magazine, copyright 1978, Ziff Davis Publishing Company.

[3] Timothy Ragan and Norman Lambert, "More About Recruitment" in *Baptist Leader* (September, 1976), p. 6.

[4] Naylor, *op. cit.*, p. 45.

[5] As stressed before, it is important to meet a volunteer's personal areas of training needs before training will be meaningful and effective. A helpful tool for identifying personal needs is Evelyn Huber's book, *Enlist, Train, Support Church Leaders* (Valley Forge: Judson Press, 1975).

[6] Huber, *op. cit.*, p. 8.

[7] Two useful resources for team building are: Nancy Geyer and Shirley Noll, *Team Building in Church Groups* (Valley Forge: Judson Press, 1970) and J. William Pfeiffer and John E. Jones, *A Handbook of Structured Experiences for Human Relations Training*, vols. 1-6 (La Jolla: University Associates, 1973-1975).

Chapter 6

[1] Ted W. Engstrom and Edward R. Dayton, *The Art of Management for Christian Leaders* (Waco, Texas: Word Books, 1976), p. 70. Used by permission of Word Books, Publisher, Waco, TX 76703.

Chapter 7

[1] Harriet H. Naylor, *Volunteers Today: Finding, Training and Working with Them* (Dryden, N.Y.: Dryden Associates, 1973), p. 110.

[2] Roy H. Ryan, *Educational Ministry with Adults* (Nashville: The Board of Education, United Methodist Church, 1972), p. 42. Copyright 1972 by the Board of Education of the United Methodist Church. Used by permission of Discipleship Resources, P.O. Box 840, Nashville, TN 37202.

Bibliography

VOLUNTEERISM

McDonough, Reginald M., *Working with Volunteer Leaders in the Church*. Nashville: Broadman Press, 1976. A general introduction to volunteers and working with volunteers in the church setting. Deals with the processes of enlistment, training, motivation, communication, and other topics of interest to administrators of volunteers.

National Board of the YMCA, *Training Volunteer Leaders—A Handbook*. 1974. Very practical and usable learning models for training experiences. A comprehensive training program for volunteers.

Naylor, Harriet, *Volunteers Today: Finding, Training and Working with Them*. Dryden, N.Y.: Dryden, Associates, 1973. A "how to" book for persons who work with volunteers. Principles, practices, and insights for the supervision and administration of volunteers and volunteer programs.

Wilson, Marlene, *The Effective Management of Volunteer Programs*. Volunteer Management Associates, 1976. This book takes the five management functions and adapts them to volunteer organizations.

ENLISTMENT AND LEADERSHIP DEVELOPMENT

Board of Education, The United Methodist Church, *Leader*

Development Resource System. 1972. A series of eight very helpful and useful handbooks for the total program of enlistment and training.

Division of Local Church Education, Board of Education of the United Methodist Church, *Enlisting and Training Leaders,* 1972. A part of the series "Innovations in Education" or innovation referral service. This is a packet of reports from local churches as to methods they have tried in recruitment and training. Names and addresses and size of church are given for follow-up.

Engstrom, Ted W., and Dayton, Edward R., *The Art of Management for Christian Leaders.* Waco, Texas: Word Books, 1976. This book takes the management principles and relates them to the church and church leadership. A good resource for pastors and others in supervision or management areas of the church.

Geyer, Nancy, and Noll, Shirley, *Team Building in Church Groups.* Valley Forge: Judson Press, 1970. Skill shops for team development. Practical suggestions for helping persons function more effectively together.

Huber, Evelyn M., *Enlist, Train, Support Church Leaders.* Valley Forge: Judson Press, 1975. The process of assessing needs for leadership, securing the persons, and giving needed support.

Sunday School Board of the Southern Baptist Convention, *Church Leader Motivation.* This is a multimedia pack which has a filmstrip, cassette tape, and a book. A basic introduction to motivation, using the Maslow "Hierarchy of Needs."

PLANNING SKILLS

Blazier, Kenneth D., *Building an Effective Church School.* Valley Forge: Judson Press, 1976. A handbook for church school superintendents and Christian education committees. Deals with the establishment of plans, recruitment, motivation, and training of the volunteer.

Blazier, Kenneth D., and Huber, Evelyn M., *Planning Christian Education in Your Church.* Valley Forge: Judson Press, 1974. A good planning process for Christian education which can be adapted and used by any program or group within the church.

Johnson, Douglas W., *Managing Change in the Church.* New York: Friendship Press, 1974. Deals with the process of change and planning for change. Covers the sharing of different points of view in a setting of mutual concern. Good discussion questions at the end of each chapter.

GROUP LEADERSHIP SKILLS

Anderson, Philip A., *Church Meetings That Matter*. New York: United Church Press, 1965. In a nontechnical way this book presents how to have more effective meetings and more participation. Small-group understanding and the role of the leader as a participant are discussed.

Turner, Nathan W., *Effective Leadership in Small Groups*. Valley Forge: Judson Press, 1977. This book is for persons who desire to be more effective leaders of small groups, committees, boards, classes. It gives very practical and useful helps in understanding group process, development, and conflict within small groups. Presents also five workshops which could be used as training events.

CONFLICT AND PROBLEM SOLVING

Cole, Charles, *Conflict and Teaching*. Nashville: The Graded Press, 1977. A multimedia pack with cassette and eight worksheets to assist persons in handling and dealing with conflict in adult groups. This is set up for individual study, but can be adapted for group use.

"Dealing Creatively with Conflict"—Unit #3 of *Church Officer Development*. Philadelphia: The Geneva Press, imprint of Westminster Press, 1975. A workshop to help persons deal with conflict.

Dietterich, Paul, *Making a Difference*. New York: Friendship Press, 1970. A step-by-step process guide for dealing with crisis issues. Problem solving and evaluation presented in detail. Adaptable to all groups.

COMMUNICATION SKILLS

"Communication"—Unit #5 of *Church Officer Development*. Philadelphia: The Geneva Press, imprint of Westminster Press, 1975. This is a one-hour skill shop on communication skills. Very useful.

Learning to Listen. Philadelphia: The Westminster Press. A skill shop in helping persons become more effective listeners!

Perrow, Maxwell V., *Effective Christian Communication*. Atlanta, Ga.: John Knox Press, 1962. A brief (47 pages) introduction to communication and the communication process. Also deals with the religious message, communication via symbols, and tools for effective communication. This book is a companion to a Cathedral filmstrip by the same name.

Powell, John, S. J., *Why Am I Afraid to Tell You Who I Am?* Niles, Ill.: Argus Communications, 1969. This book develops insight on self-awareness, personal growth, nonverbal and interpersonal communications. A good book for a person or group that wishes to grow and study why we communicate the way we do.

ADULT LEARNING

Jacobs, Norman, *Toward Effective Teaching: Adults*. Anderson, Ind.: Warner Press, Inc., 1970. A very good introduction to adults and adult education processes.

Ryan, Roy H., *Educational Ministries with Adults*. The Board of Education, United Methodist Church, 1972. A short introduction of adults and the learning process.

Appendixes

APPENDIX A

SKILL FORM FOR SUPERVISORS

Directions:

1. In column "A" place the skills in priority (1–17) as to your feeling of importance. #1 is highest and #17 lowest.
2. In column "B" put a check (✓) in those areas in which you feel confident.
3. In column "C" place an "X" in those areas you would like to work on in the coming year. (Note: it may be an area in which you now feel confident but wish to learn more.)
4. Look at those items marked with "X" and decide on three (3) that you wish to work on first. In column "D" place those three in priority: 1, 2, 3.

A	SKILLS	B	C	D	COMMENTS
	Public Speaking				
	Planning				
	Decision Making/Problem Solving				
	Interpersonal Communications				
	Discovering the Needs of Others				
	Understanding Group Process				
	Conflict Management				
	Peer Counseling				
	Faith Sharing				
	Giving Clear Directions				
	Goal Setting				
	Leading Discussions				
	Listening				
	Delegation of Work				
	Leading Group Meetings				
	Organizing				
	Asking Questions				

APPENDIX B

POSITION DESCRIPTION
BOARD OF DEACONS
FOWLER BAPTIST CHURCH

COMPENSATION: Serve to glorify God.
"Do your work, not for mere pay, but from a real desire to serve. And when the Chief Shepherd appears, you will receive the glorious crown which will never lose its brightness."

1 Peter 5:2*a,* 4 (TEV)

BASIC FUNCTIONS: Responsible for the development and administration of programs dealing with—
1. Christian Education
2. Evangelism and Missions
3. Worship
4. Church Membership

DUTIES
Constitutional
1. Aid the pastor in the performance of his duties.
2. Administer and organize the ordinance of the Lord's Supper and baptism.
3. Provide Christian instruction and ministry for the church.
4. Serve a term of three (3) years.

Other
1. Provide pulpit supply in the absence of the pastor.
2. Serve on one of the four committees of the Board.
3. Attend monthly meetings.
4. Meet with prospective new members.
5. Host Deacons' meeting when called upon.
6. Support all functions of the church.
7. Work with the pastor in the appraisal of the general well-being of the church and in the performance of the pastor's duties.
8. Supervise the extended session for children during worship.
9. Provide a nursery worker during worship.

QUALIFICATIONS
Constitutional
1. Church membership

Spiritual
   1. Born-again believer.
   2. Spiritual insight.
   3. Familiarity with Scriptures.

Other
   1. Trustworthiness.
   2. Administrative ability.

SUPERVISION
   1. Develop policies dealing with the entire educational program of the church.
   2. Choir director.
   3. Organist.
   4. Worship in general.

AUTHORITY
   1. Approve all vacations and absences of the pastor.
   2. Approve pulpit supply to be used in the pastor's absence.
   3. Approve all expenditures from the Deacon Fund.
   4. Develop and approve outreach programs.
   5. Develop and approve mission programs.
   6. Develop and approve evangelism programs.
   7. Recommend persons for church membership.
   8. Review the church membership list.

CONTACTS
Internal
   1. Greet participants after worship.
   2. Make membership aware of special needs of other members and special crisis situations.
   3. Serve as a support unit for new members.

EXTERNAL
   1. Make all visitors welcome.
   2. Make others aware of God's Good News as expressed through Christ Jesus and his church.

APPENDIX C

MUTUAL AGREEMENT OF SERVICE FORM
You Are Invited

The Board of Christian Education of _____ invites
(church)

_____ to serve as _____ in the church
(name)   (role)

school from _____ to _____.
(month/year)   (month/year)

WHAT YOUR CHURCH EXPECTS OF YOU

- A growing awareness of God and response to God through faith and love.

- A commitment to the task of the church.

- Faithful use of your skills and abilities in helping persons learn and develop as Christians.

- Thorough preparation for your weekly duties.

- Regular attendance and early arrival at church school sessions and planning meetings.

- Participation in training sessions for the church school staff.

- Cooperation with co-workers of the church school.

- Self-improvement through reading and study.

- Openness to others and to other points of view.

-

-

WHAT YOU CAN EXPECT OF YOUR CHURCH

- Worship, study, and growth experiences for your personal development.
- Periodic orientation and training sessions.
- Resources to help you in your task, including:
  —Resource people, such as the pastor, superintendents, board of Christian education, and other leaders, for special help and counsel.
  —Curriculum materials.
  —Other materials for classroom, administrative, and personal enrichment use.
  —Facilities, equipment, and supplies.
- Opportunities to participate in planning for the church school.
- Recognition of your work as vital in the life and ministry of our church.
-
-

OUR AGREEMENT

As we enter into this agreement before God, together we shall work toward our goals for the church school.

I accept the invitation to serve in the church school, and will endeavor to live up to the church's expectations of me.

Thank you for accepting the invitation. We will endeavor to make your expectations of the church become reality.

_____

Signature,
Church School Leader

_____

Signature,
Church School Superintendent

_____

Signature, Chairperson,
Board of Christian Education

_____

Signature,
Pastor

(Reprinted with permission from Kenneth D. Blazier, _Building an Effective Church School_ [Valley Forge: Judson Press, 1976])

APPENDIX D

(This is a copy of an informational system developed by one church. Other systems may be obtained through denominational book-stores.)

HUMAN RESOURCE INVENTORY

WHY THIS INFORMATION IS DESIRED: Our time, talents, abilities, and skills are really GIFTS to us from God. To be meaningful stewards of God's gifts means that they should be used and not stored away or left to die (see Matthew 25:14-30).

One place in which our gifts can be used is within the church and its ministry! The Personnel Committee of our church is trying to determine the Human Resources (gifts) within our church so that our church might make the best use of God's gifts in our present and future ministry.

Your cooperation in filling out this inventory would be most helpful. Filling out this inventory does not necessarily commit you to serving, but it gives the Personnel Committee a better understanding of the Human Resources (God's gifts) within our church.

1. NAME _____ DATE _____

2. OCCUPATION _____

3. ORGANIZATIONS OUTSIDE OF THE CHURCH IN WHICH YOU PARTICIPATE _____

    _____

4. TALENTS/ABILITIES (Please check (✓) all those areas in which you have some talent or ability.)

___Singing	___Office Work	___Drama
___Public Speaking	___Leading	___Acting
___Teaching	Recreation	___Directing
___Leading Bible Study	___Playing an Instrument	___Writing
___Leading Small Groups	___Piano	___Crafts (be specific)
___Cooking	___Organ	_____
	___Guitar	___Leading Singing

5. INTERESTS (Please check (✓) all those areas of interest to you. Space is provided to add any additional areas of interest to you.)

____Singing

____Teaching:

    ____Preschool

    ____Children

    ____Youth

    ____Young-
        Adult

    ____Adult

____Helping in
    Worship

____Ushering

____Leading
    Recreation

____Leading Singing

____Greeting

____ _____

____Serving on:

    ____Trustee

    ____Deacon

    ____Christian
        Ed.

    ____Worship

    ____Evangelism

    ____Mission

    ____Social
        Concerns

____Visiting:

    ____Visitors

    ____New
        Members

    ____Shut-ins

____ _____

____Crafts (general)

____Camp Counselor

____Family
    Education

____Drama

____Office Work

____Audiovisual

____Transportation

____Singing (solo)

____Organizing
    (dinners, etc.)

____Small-Group
    Leader

____Bible Study
    Leader

____ _____

____ _____

6. SPECIAL TRAINING. Please list all training that you have had, either professional or otherwise:

_____

_____

7. HOBBIES. Please list your hobbies: _____

_____

8. OTHER. Please list any interest or ability that has been missed:

_____

_____

9. I would be interested in using my God-given gifts in service!
    ____YES   ____NO

APPENDIX E

HUMAN RESOURCE BANK

NAME	SKILL/ABILITY	Y	N	SPECIAL TRAINING	Y	N
HUMAN RESOURCE BANK INSTRUCTIONS: List all persons and their various skills, abilities, interests, and special training. Check "Y" if that skill or training is being used. Check "N" if that skill or training is not being used.						
1. Mary Allen	Drawing		X	Commercial Art	X	
Mary Allen	Singing/solo and lead	X				
2. Bill Brown				Small Group Work	X	
3. Fred Clark	Good adult teacher	X				
4. Peter Douglas	Works well with youth	X		Management	X	
5. Jane Evans	Plays piano and guitar		X			
Jane Evans				Preschool Teacher	X	
6.						

APPENDIX F

INVENTORY OF LEADERSHIP NEEDS

YEARLY ELECTED OR APPOINTED POSITIONS	PERSON NOW SERVING	MAY BE ASKED TO SERVE AGAIN		EVALUATION OR COMMENTS ABOUT PERFORMANCE	NEED	
		yes	no		yes	no
1. Moderator	1. Jayne Smith	X		1. Jayne is doing an excellent job as Moderator and it would be worthwhile to have her continue.	X	
2. Clerk	2. James Miller	X		2. Jim has missed over half of the meetings. Should be replaced by someone who has interest and the time.	X	
3. Treasurer						
4. Head Usher						
5. Church School						
5a. Adult	5a. Tom Jones	X		5a. Tom has asked to change classes to a younger group.	X	
5b. Preschool	5b. Wilma Stein		X	5b. Wilma is a good teacher but has now taught for 3 years and should have a year off.	X	
THREE-YEAR TERMS						
1. Trustees	1a. May Smith	X		1a. May is doing a good job. We need a woman on this board.		X

APPENDIX G

A Personal Training Program

Instructions
1. IDENTIFYING TRAINING NEEDS
   Fill in one of the surveys that will help you pinpoint and identify your needs for future development and training.

2. MEETING WITH TRAINING SUPERVISOR
   Meet with your Training Supervisor (pastor, associate pastor, minister of education, superintendent, etc.) and discuss your training needs survey. Identify the area that you wish to work on developing.
   Establish a training goal—what you want to happen and what you want to learn.

3. TRAINING PROGRAM
   The Training Supervisor then will work to develop a training program to meet your goal and your needs.

4. SETTING A TRAINING SCHEDULE (time and place for meeting with your Training Supervisor).
   An important part of personal training is the one-to-one discussion time with your Training Supervisor. Set up a regular meeting time for discussion and evaluation of your learning experiences. Establish a deadline for the accomplishment of your learning goal.

TRAINING AGREEMENT

NAME _SALLY GARCIA_   POSITION _MODERATOR_

TRAINING SUPERVISOR _D·B HEUSSER, PASTOR_

TRAINING NEED _SKILL IN GROUP LEADERSHIP/SELF·CONFIDENCE_

TRAINING GOAL _TO BECOME A BETTER SKILLED AND_

MORE CONFIDENT CHURCH MODERATOR

TRAINING STEPS:
1. 1/15—meet with Training Supervisor and review Job Description and total church organizational structure.

2. Read article from December, 1977, *Baptist Leader,* "Using God's Gifts in Leadership," by Evelyn M. Huber.
3. Read the book *The Person Who Chairs the Meeting,* by Paul O. Madsen.
4. 3/1—meet with Training Supervisor to discuss the article, book, and other learnings.
5. Attend area training session at Fowler Baptist Church, 3/31.
   Attend sessions: Chairing/Leading a Meeting
   Working with Volunteers in the Church
   Creative Conflict
6. Meet with Training Supervisor to discuss the 3/31 sessions on 4/7.
7. Read *Effective Leadership for Today's Church,* by Arthur M. Adams.
8. 5/1—meet with Training Supervisor to discuss Adams's book.
9. Rewrite your Job Description in your own terms.
10. At June meeting of the church ask for some evaluation of your leadership: For example, "In what areas am I functioning well?" "In what areas can I improve my leadership?"
11. After the June meeting—meet with Training Supervisor to discuss feelings and responses from the evaluation.
12. Read *Church Meetings That Matter,* by Philip A. Anderson.
13. 7/7—meet with Training Supervisor to discuss Anderson's book and to evaluate your training experience.

I agree to work with ___**D - B**___ as my Training Supervisor and I will be faithful in my attendance at meetings and in the work that I have agreed to do.

Sally Garcia
(Trainee)

As a Training Supervisor, I agree to work with **SALLY** ___and will be faithful in attendance at meetings and in the work that I have agreed to do.

DB. Heusser
(Training Supervisor)

APPENDIX H

WORKSHOP EVALUATION FORM

What I expected to learn at this workshop was: _____

_____

_____

I feel I accomplished: ___0%, ___25%, ___50%, ___75%, ___100% of my expectations for this workshop.

The most valuable part of the workshop was: _____

_____

_____

The least helpful part was: _____

_____

_____

The part I would like to spend more time working on and learning more about: _____

_____

_____

I would rate the leader:

PREPARATION	__A	__B	__C	__D	__F
PRESENTATION	__A	__B	__C	__D	__F
COMMUNICATION	__A	__B	__C	__D	__F

Comments? Suggestions? _____

_____

_____

If you want to sign, please do. If you don't want to sign, it's OK!

APPENDIX I

VOLUNTEER EVALUATION FORM

NAME _____ POSITION _____
EVALUATOR _____ POSITION _____
Number of times the evaluator has observed volunteer this past year.
_____

In what situation/circumstances was the volunteer observed? ____
_____

INSTRUCTIONS: Step #1—Fill in the complete evaluation form, being as specific as possible. Step #2—Discuss the evaluation form with the volunteer. Be SPECIFIC and POSITIVE. Remember this should be a learning tool to assist the volunteer in his or her future development and growth.

THIS IS THE BASIC STANDARD FOR EVALUATION.
1. Check (✓) the proper evaluation of the volunteer.
   U   = Unsatisfactory: The performance/attitude is extremely deficient.
   F   = Fair: The performance/attitude must improve to be satisfactory.
   S   = Satisfactory: The performance/attitude meets all requirements.
   VG = Very Good: The performance/attitude is beyond the standards for a satisfactory performance.
   E   = Excellent: The performance/attitude is extraordinary and far beyond the basic requirement.

	U	F	S	VG	E
Effectiveness in dealing with people					
Knowledge of the job					
Initiative					
Judgment in decisions and actions					
Dependability					
Attitude toward job					
Quality of work					
Desire to learn					
Ability to communicate					
Ability to plan					
Ability to get others involved					
Fulfillment of job description					
Fulfillment of job contract/agreement					
OVERALL EVALUATION					

2.   In places you rated "U" or "F," please now indicate your reasons:

_____

_____

_____

_____

_____

_____

3. What *specific* recommendations for change or training would help the volunteer change the "U" or "F" to a satisfactory evaluation?

_____

_____

_____

_____

_____

4. What outstanding abilities and accomplishments have you noted in the volunteer? _____

_____

_____

5. In what ways can you, as a supervisor, be of greater assistance to the volunteer? _____

_____

_____

_____

6. Would you recommend that the volunteer continue in the same position or make a change to a different position? Why? ____

_____

_____

_____

7. Comments: _____

_____

_____

8. Discuss this evaluation with the volunteer!